A Portrait of
New Zealand

A Portrait of
New Zealand

Photographs by Robin Smith & Warren Jacobs
Text by Errol Brathwaite

KOWHAI

Contents

SOUTH ISLAND

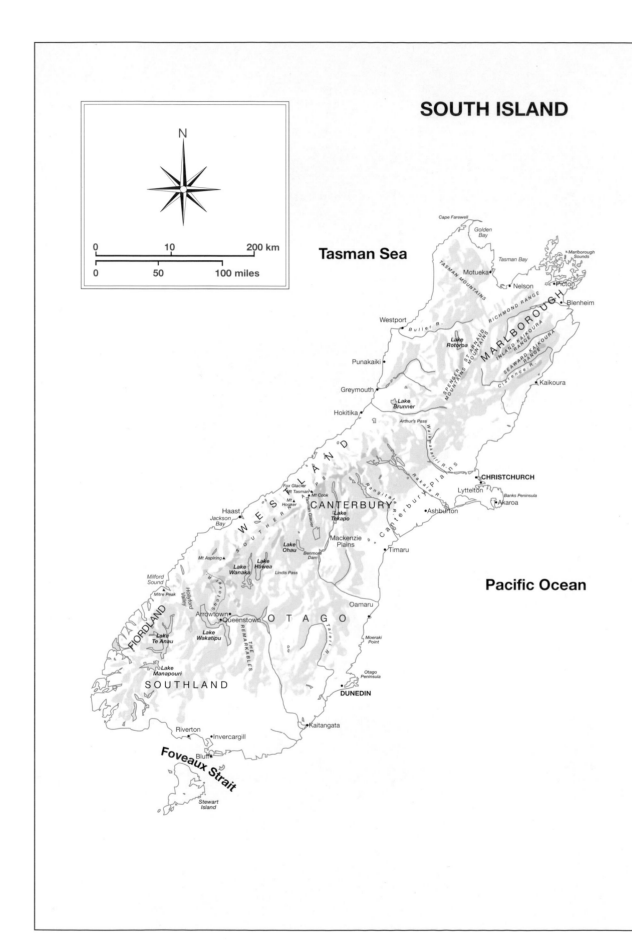

Tasman Sea

Pacific Ocean

Cape Farewell
Golden Bay
Marlborough Sounds
Tasman Bay
Motueka
Nelson
Picton
Blenheim

TASMAN MOUNTAINS
RICHMOND RANGE
MARLBOROUGH
INLAND KAIKOURA RANGE
SEAWARD KAIKOURA RANGE

Westport
Buller R.
Lake Rotoroa

SPENSER MOUNTAINS
ST. ARNAUD MOUNTAINS

Punakaiki
Clarence R.
Kaikoura

Greymouth
Lake Brunner

Hokitika
Arthur's Pass

Waimakariri R.

CHRISTCHURCH
Lyttelton
Banks Peninsula
Akaroa

Rakaia R.
Canterbury Plains
Rangitata R.
Ashburton

Fox Glacier
Mt Tasman
Mt Cook
Mt Hooker
Tasman Glacier

W E S T L A N D
S O U T H E R N   A L P S

CANTERBURY
Lake Tekapo

Haast
Jackson Bay

Lake Ohau
Mackenzie Plains
Benmore Dam
Timaru

Mt Aspiring
Lake Wanaka
Lake Hawea
Lindis Pass

Milford Sound
Mitre Peak

Haast R.
Hollyford Valley

Oamaru

Arrowtown
Queenstown
O T A G O
THE REMARKABLES

Taieri R.

Moeraki Point

FIORDLAND
Lake Te Anau
Lake Wakatipu

Otago Peninsula

Lake Manapouri
S O U T H L A N D

DUNEDIN

Riverton
Invercargill
Kaitangata

Bluff

Foveaux Strait

Stewart Island

Scale
0   10   200 km
0   50   100 miles
N

NORTH ISLAND

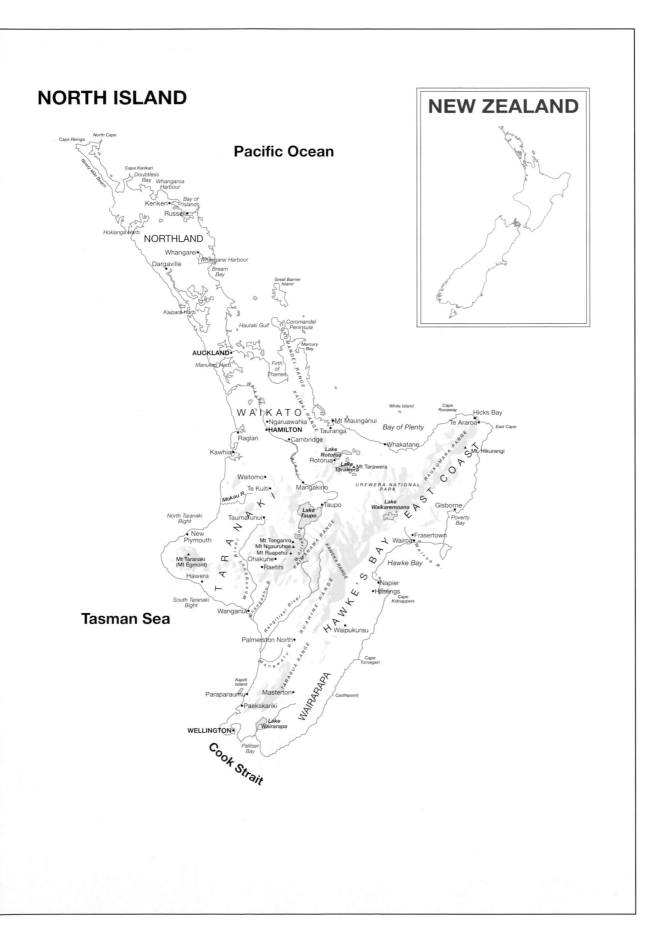

NEW ZEALAND

Pacific Ocean

North Cape
Cape Reinga
Ninety Mile Beach
Cape Karikari
Doubtless Bay
Whangaroa Harbour
Kerikeri
Bay of Islands
Russell
Hokianga Harb.
NORTHLAND
Whangarei
Dargaville
Whangarei Harbour
Bream Bay
Great Barrier Island
Kaipara Harb.
Hauraki Gulf
Coromandel Peninsula
AUCKLAND
Mercury Bay
Manukau Harb.
COROMANDEL RANGE
Firth of Thames
KAIMAI RANGE
WAIKATO
White Island
Cape Runaway
Hicks Bay
•Mt Maunganui
Te Araroa
Ngaruawahia
HAMILTON
Tauranga
East Cape
Raglan
Cambridge
Bay of Plenty
Kawhia
•Whakatane
Lake Rotorua
Rotorua
RAUKUMARA RANGE
Mt Hikurangi
Waitomo
Lake Tarawera
Mt Tarawera
EAST COAST
Te Kuiti
Mangakino
UREWERA NATIONAL PARK
Mokau R.
Taupo
Lake Waikaremoana
Gisborne
TARANAKI
North Taranaki Bight
Taumarunui
Lake Taupo
Poverty Bay
New Plymouth
Mt Tongariro
Mt Ngauruhoe
Mt Ruapehu
Frasertown
Wairoa
Mt Taranaki (Mt Egmont)
Ohakune
•Raetihi
KAIMANAWA RANGE
KAWEKA RANGE
Hawke Bay
Wairoa R.
Hawera
Whanganui River
Whangaehu R.
RUAHINE RANGE
•Napier
•Hastings
Cape Kidnappers
South Taranaki Bight
Wanganui
Rangitikei River
HAWKE'S BAY
Waipukurau
Tasman Sea
Manawatu River
Palmerston North
Cape Turnagain
Kapiti Island
TARARUA RANGE
Paraparaumu
Masterton
WAIRARAPA
Castlepoint
Paekakariki
Lake Wairarapa
WELLINGTON
Palliser Bay
Cook Strait

9

North Island

A Volcanic Heritage

ACCORDING to Maori tradition the North Island of New Zealand was a fish, caught by the demi-god Maui. The canoe from which he caught this fish became the South Island, with Stewart Island as its anchor stone. This story sets the North Island atmosphere perfectly, because the hauling up of a fish of such prodigious size suggests of Homeric spectacle – and the North Island is spectacular. It also suggests mystery, because how a people who knew no maps managed to perceive the fish-like shape of an island some 1000km (620 miles) long is a mystery, the answer to which is buried deep in Maori lore.

The tale goes on to tell of how Maui's brothers, half crazed with hunger, leaped onto the monstrous fish and began to devour it raw, so that it is gouged and scarred, and its backbone is exposed; and the picture thus conjured up is indeed a fair enough depiction of the North Island's highlands.

Visitors to New Zealand, coming first to the North Island, sometimes express surprise at the fact that they see no high alps and no mighty glaciers, though such features often fill New Zealand's commercial travel literature almost to the exclusion of all else. Yet few such comments reveal any sense of disappointment. On the contrary, the ecstatic visitor usually finds fresh evidence each day that what the North Island lacks in scenic grandeur, it makes up for in sheer spectacle. For this is a land in which the creative forces of nature are still awesomely at work. The same applies in the South Island; but where the Southern Alps have been pushed up gradually, over aeons of time, by the infinitely ponderous movement of the plates of the earth's fractured crust, the highest mountains of the North Island have often leaped into being, or have suddenly disappeared, sometimes within remembered history, as the result or aftermath of violent explosions.

The same is true of many of the lakes and rivers. Where the South Island's alpine lakes have formed slowly in valleys carved by ice-age glaciers, many North Island lakes began as massive subsidences due to earthquakes or subterranean upheavals.

COROMANDEL RANGE, NEAR COROGLEN

This high range runs along the Coromandel Peninsula and its highest peaks are over 800m (2625ft). Exquisitely beautiful forest grows from the valleys where the ridges dovetail into one another, right to the tops, with tree ferns and podocarps, and stands of the lordly kauri. The forest is alive with tui and fantail, grey warbler and the friendly native pigeon. The range is traversed by roads which wind around rocky spurs and frequently dive into deep, shady and now peaceful valleys, where men once milled the timber, and probed and dug for precious kauri gum.

Today's main route from Raetihi, west of Ohakune, to Wanganui, on the western coast, accompanies the Mangawhero River. The name means 'Red Stream', so called from the red algae which coats rocks on its banks. Though it runs for much of its length through tamed pasture land, it still has along its banks a thin fringe of native bush. The Ruawaka Falls, dropping suddenly over a bush-screened shelf, may have been the scene of ancient tragedies, for the name means 'Pit for Canoes'.

RIGHT: MT TARANAKI AND LAKE MANGAMAHOE

Mt Taranaki, for long thought to be an extinct volcano, is now known to be merely dormant. It once had a twin peak, which shattered in some cataclysmic explosion, and the tangle of forested hills between the mountain and the city of New Plymouth is its torn remnant. Lake Mangamahoe's name suggests a contradiction, because 'Manga' means 'stream', but that is precisely what this lake once was, before it was dammed to form an artificial lake, some 30-odd hectares in area, supplying New Plymouth with water and electricity.

Where pressure-folding has produced mountain ranges, the result stands for all to see – but the cause, being infinitely slow, is imperceptible, and some North Island ranges are still rising. So slow is the process, however, that the Manawatu River, which rises on the eastern side of the island's 'backbone' mountain chain, flows out to the west coast, wearing its way down as fast as the range rises, creating a deep gorge and separating the mountain wall into two distinct and separate ranges, the Ruahines and the Tararuas.

But where volcano, earthquake, rockfall and subsidence are the creators of the landscape, the cause is usually still visible. On a clear day, from an aeroplane, the volcanic fault-line may be easily discerned in the rift-valleys, and in the long chain of volcanic peaks, steaming lakes, fumaroles and active volcanoes that stretches diagonally from White Island, the ferocious, Etna-like volcano out in the Bay of Plenty, to the central volcanic plateau. The force which shaped this landscape, which collapsed it, tossed it, tumbled and tangled it, is still there, still visible, still working, still smoking and steaming and filling the air with its sulphurous breath.

The largest visible subsidence area is right in the middle of the island. The waters of a major river and a dozen other sizeable streams flow into it, to form New Zealand's largest lake, Lake Taupo, 41km (25 miles) long and up to 27km (17 miles) wide, with a total area of 616 square km (238 square miles). New Zealand's longest river, the Waikato, 434km (270 miles) long, flows out of the north-eastern end of the lake.

The North Island's mountains do not compare in size with those of the Southern Alps. Highest is Mt Ruapehu, 2797m (9175ft), about 58th in the list of New Zealand's highest mountains, yet quite high enough to have snow on its

ABOVE: HUKA FALLS, WAIKATO RIVER
The young Waikato River comes away from Lake Taupo across level land, only to slip, as it were, on a sloping, rocky scarp which has been split by some gigantic earthquake. For some 200m (656ft), it slides down, ever more narrowly confined, ever gathering momentum, bullying its way past great boulders, plucking at riverside vegetation, until it makes its 10-metre (33-ft) leap over the Huka Falls in an earth-shaking display of power.

peak all year round; and what it lacks in height, it makes up for in wonder, with its crater lake steaming hot, though surrounded by ice and snow to its very edge.

North Islanders, like South Islanders, seldom live out of sight of the mountains, though there are some exceptions. In Northland there are steep, rugged hills which, in some older lands, would doubtless be labelled 'mountains', but which are not exceptionally high in rugged New Zealand, and are never snow-crowned, but have forested tops. But in almost every other part of New Zealand's North Island, mountains dominate the skyline, along a great chain which runs from Mt Hikurangi, 1752m (5747ft), often claimed to be the first peak in New Zealand to be lit by the rising sun. The mountain chain runs down through the Raukumara Range, the Kaweka Range, the tangled massif of the Kaimanawas, the curving wall of the Ruahine Range, and the steep Tararuas. Rising in a long curve southward from the base of the Coromandel Peninsula is the Kaimai Range, forested to its tops; and branching from the edge of the volcanic plateau is a vast area of crumpled high-country, densely forested, which

Above: Tongariro River

The Tongariro River rises on the eastern flanks of Mt Ruapehu, in Tongariro National Park. It is, somewhat confusingly, known as the Upper Waikato from its source to where it is joined by the Waihohonu Stream. From this point to where it flows into Lake Taupo it is known officially as the Tongariro River. There is less confusion, however, in its reputation as a trout stream. Anglers world-wide consider it without a doubt the best fishing river in New Zealand, and one of the finest in the world.

Left: trout, Rainbow Springs, Rotorua

Rainbow Springs (and the nearby Fairy Springs) are famous for the crystal clarity of the water, and the fat trout which inhabit them. A path wanders alongside the stream, slightly below it, and underwater viewing windows allow visitors to observe the giant (and captive) brown trout closely. Welling springs uplift grains of white pumice and black obsidian – for this is on the volcanic fault line – which colour the water a lovely shade of blue.

17

PREVIOUS PAGE RIGHT: MANGAWHERO RIVER, NEAR OHAKUNE

From the south-western slopes of Mt Ruapehu, the Mangawhero River fights its way over a boulder-strewn, scrub-covered, volcanic landscape, running into heavy bush as it sweeps past Raetihi and Ohakune, accompanying the Parapara Gorge route between Raetihi and Wanganui, and thrusting at last into the Whangaehu River. Even in the peaceful calm of the forest, away from the rifted landscape around its parent mountain, it surges forward with impatient power, crashing past ancient, mossy boulders, and overwhelming ridges and upthrustings of rock.

PREVIOUS PAGE ABOVE LEFT: EVENING LIGHT, MT RUAPEHU

The sun, setting in a blaze of rose-coloured glory, bathes the great bulk of Mt Ruapehu in a pink glow, and touches with red the snow-patched tussock in the grim desert of pumice soil at the volcano's feet. The biggest of three volcanic mountains on the central plateau, Ruapehu stands 2797m (9175ft), a broken, truncated cone which was once much higher. Recent periods of volcanic activity have served as dramatic reminders of the forces of nature still at work in this mountain.

PREVIOUS PAGE BELOW LEFT: RAINBOW FALLS, KERIKERI, BAY OF ISLANDS

On the lower reaches of the Kerikeri River, about 5km (3 miles) upstream from where it runs out into its sheltered inlet, the placid, narrow, meandering stream takes a sudden dramatic plunge over a rocky ledge. The falls usually have a fragile veil of spray which, when it catches the sun's rays, paints a rainbow across the basin into which the water falls. The white water, the rainbow and the surrounding filigree of greenery are an exquisite little cameo in a landscape where even the clay in the roadside banks is tinted a delicate rose pink; for this is, or was, a volcanic countryside.

ABOVE: HUKA RAPIDS

Some 200m (656 ft) upstream from the Huka Falls, the Waikato River slips on an inclined shelf of rock and slides down, dropping about 9m (30 ft) in that distance. It gathers speed as it races down to the head of the Huka Falls, clutching at the sides of the cleft, crashing over boulders, twisting, turning, tumbling, never in the whole of its length displaying more power than it does here, yet confined to a width of a mere 15m (50ft). Huka means 'foam', and the rapids certainly live up to that name, especially where the river plunges at last down some 10m (33 ft), a maelstrom of turquoise-green and white foam.

ABOVE: THE WAIROA RIVER

The Wairoa River is a mere 80km (50 miles) in length, yet within that short compass it is one of the most complex river systems in New Zealand. The Waiau River, flowing south-eastwards, is swelled by the waters of the Waikaretaheke, which drains Lake Waikaremoana, and joins the Wairoa near Frasertown. The Ruakituri and Hangaroa Rivers run down from the north-west into the Wairoa, and the Mangapoike Stream joins it from the north-east. The result is a broad, smoothly flowing river watering a rich, alluvial countryside around the town of Wairoa. Navigable for about 23km (15 miles) from its mouth, it made the little town a minor port in the days before road and rail reached it from north and south.

which rises at its western edge up to the slopes of Mt Taranaki (also known as Mt Egmont), 2518m (8260ft).

Though they are not as high or as grand as the Southern Alps, it is among the mountains of the North Island that the largest, most beautiful lakes lie; and from their bush-clad flanks flow great rivers, deep and frequently navigable. On some North Island mountains there are ski-fields which are famous worldwide. Some of the mountains cradle lakeside resorts on their flanks. Others smoulder and spit and rumble menacingly, and harbour weird areas of boiling mud, geysers, silica terraces and sulphurous steam. All of them share that brooding quality of mountains, an air of dark secrecy – and they are all captivating in the extreme.

Perhaps it suffices to say that the North Island's mountains, lakes, rivers and thermal areas have a shape, an aspect, an atmosphere all of their own – and they are unsurpassed anywhere for sheer, breathtaking beauty.

Taken all in all, there is less nostalgia apparent in the North Island. There were some attempts to reproduce something of the homeland which the first settlers left to come here, but nothing to compare with, say, the almost aggressive Englishness of Christchurch or the equally determined Scottishness of Dunedin. Always there is a frank, if enforced, acknowledgement of the fact that the settlers and their culture were a transplant. You see it in public gardens, like the Lady Norwood Rose Garden in Wellington, where the dainty flowers, in their straight and formal rows, bloom against a background of cheerfully unkempt native shrubs and trees. You are made aware of it by towns which were named after English localities, but which, in time, reverted to the Maori name for the place, even though the streets, in good English fashion, retain the names of past aldermen, famous generals and Empire dignitaries.

ABOVE: PANEKIRI BLUFF, LAKE WAIKAREMOANA

The Panekiri Range rises up on one side of Lake Waikaremoana, with peaks over 1100m (3600ft) high, and runs north-eastwards to terminate in this high and dramatic bluff that drops into the lake. The beautiful, star-shaped lake lies in the Urewera highlands, at an altitude of 614m (2015ft) above sea level, surrounded by densely forested mountains. Formed by an ancient rock-fall which blocked the path of the Waikaretaheke River, it is some 54 sq km (21 sq miles) in area, with depths of up to 247m (810ft), and is fed by many mountain streams which come down to the lake, often over exquisite waterfalls.

RIGHT: GREEN LAKE, ROTORUA

In the twisted, fragmented, rumpled landscape south of Rotorua, on the wonderfully scenic road that goes to the Buried Village and Lake Tarawera, lie the twin lakes, Green Lake and Blue Lake. They are separated by a narrow neck of tree-covered land, and are named for the colour of their waters. The Maori name for Green Lake is Rotokakahi, which means 'lake of the kakahi' (fresh-water mussel), which the Maori found to be abundant in the lake's clear waters.

ABOVE: MT NGAURUHOE AND
WHAKAPAPANUI STREAM

Of the trio of volcanoes, Ruapehu,
Ngauruhoe and Tongariro, that rise out of
the central volcanic plateau, Mt Ngauruhoe
is the most symmetrical. Rising 2291m
(7515ft), it emerges from a shattered tangle
of craters and rifts of which it has gradually
become the dominant feature. The next
highest eminence in the complex is
Tongariro, at 1968m (6455ft). From the
flanks of Ruapehu, the largest and
southernmost peak, flows the
Whakapapanui Stream, running down
across a scrub-and-pumice landscape to join
the Whakapapa, an upper tributary of the
Whanganui River.

The culture of the settlers never really fused with the culture of the Maori. For
long, many people of both races told themselves and each other that they had;
but it is not so, and the realisation has dawned that it is better that it is not so.
As each race acknowledges its differences, respect and appreciation can go hand-
in-hand and this is beginning to happen. As it does, the fascination of the North
Island will grow, and what is at present an ingredient in its difference will become
one of its principal attractions.

ABOVE: MUD POOL

Mud pools are a source of almost endless fascination. The mud gurgles and slurps like hot porridge in a pot. One such pool at Whakarewarewa is known as the Frog Pond, because gouts of mud, thrown from bursting mud bubbles, seem to hop across the surface like small silver frogs, a phenomenon which occurs after rain when the mud is less viscous.

RIGHT: MT NGAURUHOE, TONGARIRO NATIONAL PARK

Mt Ngauruhoe is thought to have been formed about 2500 years ago, no great age for a volcano. In continuous eruption, it mostly emits gas in the form of steam, but from time to time it becomes somewhat more violent and belches forth ash. Geological records show that it spilled forth red-hot lava in 1949 and again in 1954, and in contrast to the ash explosions which last for a short time (from mere minutes to a few days), the lava outpourings are apt to go on for months. There are walking tracks in the vicinity of the cone, but it is necessary to watch closely for any sign of increasing activity, and to leave the area as quickly as possible when such signs are noticed.

ABOVE LEFT: TARAWERA VOLCANIC RENT

At 12.30am on 10 June 1886, a series of earthquakes began around Mt Tarawera, south-east of Rotorua. Then, at 1.30am, an explosion occurred on the north-eastern end of the mountain. At 1.45am, a horrendous roar burst from the vicinity of Ruawahia Peak, and a vast black column, shot with the glowing red of hot rocks, rocketed skywards. Twenty minutes later, with an even more deafening roar, the south-eastern end of the mountain burst open, throwing up a cloud which was estimated to be 10km (6 miles) high. It was followed by explosion after explosion, bellowing holocausts which were heard at Coromandel, over 161km (100 miles) distant, as a chain of craters 19km (12 miles) long ripped the mountain apart. An estimated 155 people, two Maori settlements and the European village of Te Wairoa were destroyed.

BELOW LEFT: TERRACE FORMATIONS, WHAKAREWAREWA

Terraces of silvery-white silica, streaked in many places by deposits of other minerals, are a feature of the thermal areas. The most famous terrace formation for many years, the Pink and White Terraces in the Rotomahana Basin, was destroyed by the eruption of Mt Tarawera in 1886.

ABOVE RIGHT: STEAMING CLIFFS, LAKE ROTOMAHANA

In the latter half of the nineteenth century the Rotomahana Basin, with its exquisite Pink and White Terraces, was an internationally famous tourist attraction, and one of the natural wonders of the world. The eruption of Mt Tarawera destroyed it and created a lake with large areas of boiling water bubbling up in the midst of an expanse of ordinarily cold water. Along with the Steaming Cliffs, this leaves no doubt that the lake fills a large volcanic rift.

BELOW RIGHT: MT NGAURUHOE ERUPTING

The smoke rolls down the flanks of the perfect cone, and a powdering of fine ash may spread across the country as far as Hawke's Bay to the east, across the Kaiwekas, or to the Tasman Sea coast, to colour the sunsets for days at a time. But this is not a particularly violent eruption, and there is no glowing magma being tossed high into the sky, nor any avalanches of ash and hot rock bounding down the mountainside. This eruption is merely one of the mountain's periodic grumblings.

ABOVE: CRATERS OF THE MOON, WAIRAKEI

The Wairakei Valley is an area slightly to the north of Taupo, a place of steaming pools and silica terraces, which once held a number of spectacular geysers. Today, due to the tapping of the underground steam for the Wairakei Geothermal Power scheme, they no longer erupt. But a new area has been opened up – the Craters of the Moon, which includes steaming, bubbling pits and the famed Karapiti Blowhole, a fumarole of considerable activity, as an indication of the colossal power which seethes and fumes beneath the trembling ground.

RIGHT: WAIRAKEI GEOTHERMAL POWER STATION

Steam bores, sunk into the sub-surface cauldron of the Wairakei Valley, tap the vast energy source of the thermal region, and feed the high-pressure steam to turbines in a power station which has a load capacity of some 200 megawatts, about 5% of the country's total consumption. The generators are housed in a unique building designed to withstand earthquake shocks without the turbine chamber floors being tilted or disturbed unduly.

LEFT: POHUTU GEYSER, WHAKAREWAREWA

Whakarewarewa, perhaps the best known of the Rotorua thermal parks, is on the southern edge of Rotorua city. More than 500 hot springs boil there with varying degrees of violence, and a Maori village spreads around its eastern edge, the inhabitants using the hot pools for cooking and other domestic purposes. The area is a mere 1km (^{5}/8 mile) long by 500m (545 yards) wide. The finest spectacle is the famous Pohutu Geyser, which hurls a jet of steaming water to heights of 18m (60ft) and more.

ABOVE RIGHT: WHITE ISLAND

Grumbling and steaming, 50km (30 miles) off the Bay of Plenty coast, White Island is a steadily active volcano. Tour operators take boats out to the island for guided tours (hard hats and gas masks provided!) and it is also possible to visit it by helicopter. But it is a dangerous place, with its little lakes of acid and its acid mud and occasional whiffs of toxic fumes. The floor of the crater is below sea level.

BELOW RIGHT: CHAMPAGNE POOL, WAIOTAPU

About 30km (19 miles) south of Rotorua, the Waiotapu Reserve possesses some of the finest thermal activity spectacles in the area, including the outstanding Lady Knox Geyser, the Frying Pan, Echo Lake, Chromatopsia Terraces, the Explosion Craters, Alum Cliffs, Venus Baths, Primrose Terrace and the impressive hot waterfall. The Champagne Pool is a sizeable lake which, when a handful of sand is tossed into it, bubbles like champagne, which it also approximates in colour.

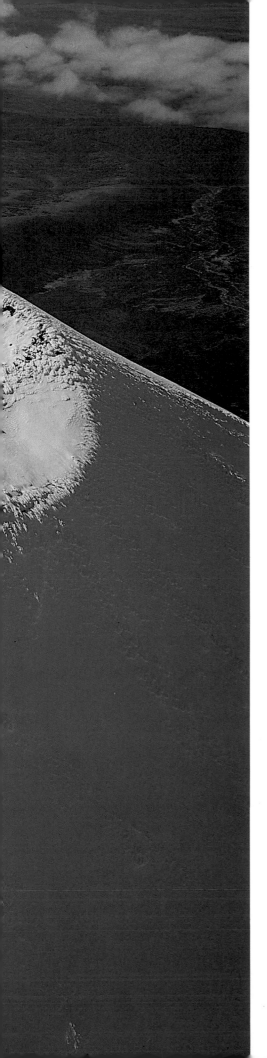

LEFT: THE SUMMIT, MT NGAURUHOE

The fascinating double crater at the top of Mt Ngauruhoe's cone is a clue to the way in which the mountain itself grew. The lovely cone rises out of the shattered multi-cratered flank of Mt Tongariro, a vent which clearly has developed into a distinct and separate mountain. On its own top, a crater within the original crater has opened up, forming a cone upon the original cone.

BELOW: THERMAL ACTIVITY, TIKITERE (HELL'S GATE)

Between Lakes Rotorua and Rotoiti is Tikitere, named 'Hell's Gate' for extra – and hardly necessary – dramatic effect. This is the most active of the thermal areas, a series of cauldrons of boiling water, seething mud, fumaroles and sulphurous steam, where the ground trembles with the pent-up power beneath the surface.

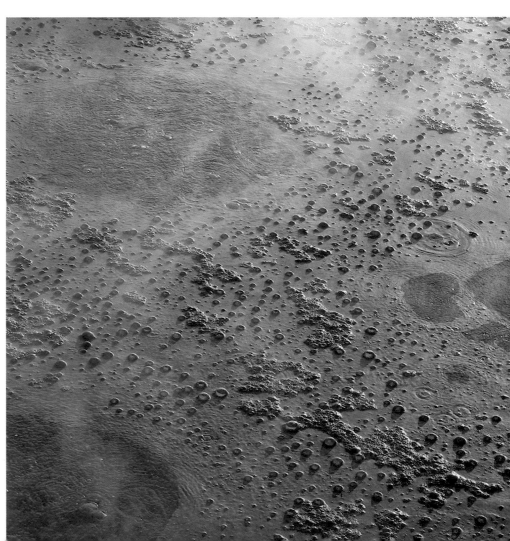

ABOVE LEFT: MOKAU STREAM AND LAKE WAIKAREMOANA

The Mokau Stream rises on the slopes of the bush-clad mountain Pukepuke (which translates oddly as Hill Hill), to the north of Lake Waikareiti. The Mokau is a swift-flowing mountain stream which flows into the Mokau Arm of Lake Waikaremoana. Near the point of entry, it drops over a great buttress of rock to form the Mokau Falls, one of the many delightful cascades in the area.

BELOW LEFT: WAIKARI RIVER, HAWKE'S BAY

Almost half way between Napier and Wairoa, perhaps 8km (5 miles) inland from the centre of the horseshoe curve of Hawke Bay, the settlement of Putorino (the name is that of a Maori flute), spreads along the banks of the Waikari River. Maori legend says that it is named from an incident in the travels of the ancient explorer, Paoa, when his dog kept on digging until he found water. But the story does the lovely stream less than justice. It is a picturesque stretch of water, where native bush and Old World willow combine to shade its pools, in a valley of great beauty.

RIGHT: KAURI TREE NEAR RUSSELL, BAY OF ISLANDS

Not the least of the attractions of the Northland bays for the old-time whalers and traders was the seemingly infinite supply of kauri trees. The kauri was huge and straight-grained. Its trunk, branchless for many metres, was tough and wonderfully durable, and made magnificent masts and spars. But it takes the kauri something like 1000 years to reach the height and maturity they preferred, and the timber-takers nearly cut it to extinction. Today it is rigidly protected.

ABOVE: KOWHAI FLOWERS

The kowhai tree is, generally speaking, a
forest-edge tree, starting life as a tiny shrub
seedling in the protecting shade of the tall
trees. Related to the broom, it is much
more spindly, and usually much taller, with
great pendant clusters of golden flowers in
season. A legume, it is part of the same
plant family as the similar, though scarlet,
kaka-beak and, perhaps surprisingly, the
common or garden pea.

RIGHT: PAPAKORITO FALLS,
WAIKAREMOANA

The Aniwaniwa (Rainbow) Stream comes
down from the bush-clad tops, tumbling
over the steep slopes of the Urewera
highlands, leaping over perpendicular walls
of rock, to the beautiful Whanganui-a-parua
Arm of Lake Waikaremoana. The best-
known cascade on this rushing stream is
that known as Aniwaniwa Falls; but scarcely
less beautiful, though smaller, is the
waterfall known as Papakorito Falls, where a
level reach of the river suddenly tumbles in
three dramatic tiers down into a tree-
shaded basin.

ABOVE: LAKE TARAWERA

The lovely road which winds past the Blue and Green Lakes, and slips discreetly past Te Wairoa, the Buried Village, dips down at last to a bush-fringed shore, on which there is a cavern containing ancient rock drawings of the Maori. And from this shore there stretches a large and beautiful lake, at the far end of which rises a truncated cone, dreadfully shattered and gashed. The lake is Lake Tarawera, and the broken mountain is Mt Tarawera, which, on 10 June 1886, exploded with devastating force, burying the little village of Te Wairoa and other lakeside settlements beneath many metres of hot ash and pumice. The surrounding countryside was ravaged and tumbled by the accompanying earthquakes, and there was a great loss of life. Today, the regenerated forest and the sheltering, enclosing hills make it difficult to imagine the devastation of that night of terror.

LEFT: ACACIA BAY, LAKE TAUPO

Boats drawn up on a beach strewn with chunks of the strange, light, porous, floating rock called pumice; the launches and yachts riding at anchor in the cove; yachts leaning like small, white pyramids far out on the lake; and the prospect of a distant shore, create a scene which belongs to the seacoast, rather than to the centre of a rugged island, some 369m (1210ft) above sea level. But that's what Lake Taupo is – an inland sea which, before the roads were pushed through, was plied by at least one steamer.

ABOVE: SUNSET OVER LAKE TAUPO AND THE VOLCANOES

Lake Taupo is New Zealand's largest lake, some 41km (25 miles) in length and 27km (17 miles) wide at its widest point. A water of many moods, it can be sparklingly inviting when the summer sun is high and the dazzling pumice beaches are hot underfoot; and it can whip up into sudden rages when the winds sweep down over the volcanic plateau and stir its waters into a dangerous turbulence. But within an hour of such a storm, when the wind dies at evening, it can lie peacefully again in a flat and dreamy calm, reflecting the sunset light from a washed sky.

ABOVE: MOKAU RIVER, NEAR TE KUITI, KING COUNTRY

This placid stream winds delightfully through meadows and between high limestone bluffs. As it meanders towards the Tasman Sea coast it grows to become one of New Zealand's finest waterways, yet one which, today, is probably the least known navigable stream in New Zealand. Just over 125km (78 miles) in length, its lower reaches flow between cliffs crowned spectacularly with forest, as fine as anything on the Whanganui River; and until the late 1920s or early 1930s, regular sea-going traffic plied upstream for some 38km (23 miles) to the one-time port of Mokau, and its coal mines.

RIGHT: GLOW-WORM GROTTO, WAITOMO CAVES

Down the centre of the North Island, and for some distance through the South Island, are vast reefs of limestone. In the Waitomo District of the King Country these are riddled with underground streams. Best known are the Waitomo Caves, a group of caverns known individually as Waitomo Cave, Ruakuri Cave and Aranui Cave. The glow-worms (actually the larval form of an insect) suspend themselves from the cave roof by a sticky thread which traps insects. Viewed from a boat in pitch darkness, the glow-worms appear as vast constellations of blue-white lights, unforgettably beautiful.

ABOVE: WHANGANUI RIVER, FROM GENTLE ANNIE HILL

The Whanganui River has been called the Rhine of New Zealand and its valley is indeed gentle with farms and dark with forest. It is navigable and was once a main highway to the interior. It even had the occasional fighting pa perched like a robber baron's castle on crags overlooking the stream. The Whanganui is 226km (140 miles) long, and the terminal port for its once considerable traffic was Taumaranui, 100 river-miles (162km) and 90 rapids inland from the river's broad mouth on the Tasman Sea coast.

RIGHT: LAKE TUTIRA, HAWKE'S BAY

Lake Tutira lies in a green basin, bush and willow-fringed, on the main road between Napier and Wairoa. The lake is the haunt of a wide variety of native and introduced waterfowl, for which it is a sanctuary. In the 1930s, the land about the lake was extensively planted with trees in a successful effort to halt erosion. Lake Tutira is separated from its smaller neighbour, Lake Waikapiro, by a narrow tongue of land, and both drain through a narrow rift into the Waikoau River.

ABOVE: LAKE WAIKAREMOANA SUNSET

Considered by many to be one of New Zealand's two most beautiful lakes (the other being the South Island's Manapouri), Waikaremoana is an intricate stretch of waterways, with inlets and islands and coves of a Garden-of-Eden-like beauty. Its bluffs stand sharply forth and forested crests are silhouetted cleanly in the crystal-clear air, constant reminders that this magnificent lake is situated in the midst of romantically wild highlands – never more so than at evening, when the tops are black against a spectacular sky.

LEFT: CRATER LAKE, MT RUAPEHU

Ruapehu is still very much an active volcano, as is Ngauruhoe's symmetrical cone, rising in the near distance. But Ruapehu, between eruptions, cradles in its snow-bound crater a sulphurous, somewhat acid lake of steaming water, which periodically disappears, to be replaced by a sullen, spitting, fuming hole which belches forth mud and ash.

ABOVE: MT RUAPEHU

From the vicinity of Ohakune, 25km (15 miles) to the south-west, Mt Ruapehu stands revealed as an awesomely broken cone, snow-covered, with broad faces providing excellent ski-fields. The longest established fields, and those best known internationally, are reached from Chateau Tongariro, but there are also comparatively newly developed fields, reached by road from Ohakune, which are growing steadily in popularity.

Nature Tamed

EVEN before the advent of Europeans, Maori had left unmistakable marks on the landscape. The North Island abounds in hills which, in tribal days, were strategically or tactically important; and these remain ridged with entrenchments, and dented with pits which once held food stores. There is, too, at least one river-mouth silted up as the result of their campaigning, when a tribe's whole fleet of sea-going vessels sank at anchor in the estuary. Here and there, ancient palisade posts mark the site of an old pa; and there are still, amongst the fern and scrub of a silent countryside, earthen forts designed to cope with bullet and cannon shell. Little else remains of the Maori's pre-European or early-European existence, because, although they planted extensive gardens and built towns with populations of up to 10 000, they lived with, not against, nature. The tribes followed nature's moods and seasons, moving from cultivation land to bird-spearing forest to fishing grounds to eeling swamps, and they took from forest, river, lake and sea only as much as they needed. The greater part of their rigidly upheld law lay in the field of conservation – 600 years before the pakeha, the white stranger, ever thought of it. Therefore, it is the pakeha who has wrought the greatest changes, in less than two centuries, stripping thousands of square miles of bush from the hills and turning them into pasture, garden, township, city and exotic forest, with road and rail, airport and harbour to link town with town and farm with farm, and tying New Zealand into the vast network of the world's commerce and communication.

This much may be said of both the North and South Islands; yet there remains a discernible difference between the impression made by the North Island settlers on their environment and the mark made by the South Island pioneers.

North Island pioneers worked no less diligently than their South Island counterparts, but their task was immeasurably harder. The two or three planned settlement schemes were less well organised, perhaps because they were generally earlier than the South Island schemes, and the colonists and the schemes' organisers had less knowledge of the conditions they would have to contend with. Further, there was a large Maori population in the North Island, and a clash was inevitable. It came, it grew and it dragged on through nearly 40 years of intermittent skirmishes and bitter warfare. Settlers saw the fruits of their prodigious labours go up in the smoke and flames of sudden raid and pitched battle.

LEFT: PASTORAL SCENE NEAR WAIPUKURAU, HAWKE'S BAY

Limestone-skeletoned hills, rolling and gentle, provide lush pastures for sheep in central Hawke's Bay. The country is well watered by myriad small creeks and streams, tributaries of the Tukituki River. Where once there was much forest, and swamp-filled valleys, the settlers created an almost European landscape of willow and poplar and pine, with small neat towns, and hillsides ridged and terraced by the feet of a million sheep. This is some of the richest pastoral land in New Zealand.

ABOVE: WAIRARAPA PASTORAL SCENE, NEAR
MASTERTON

Masterton, at the northern end of the
Wairarapa Plain, is the administrative centre
of Wairarapa County. Between Masterton
and the coast, the plain gives way to rolling
hills and twisting valleys, well-watered,
fertile, and giving lush grazing to a huge
number of sheep.

RIGHT: FARMLANDS, TARAWERA

The farmlands of Tarawera are relatively
new. A volcanic countryside, once a
wasteland of pumice- and ash-covered soil,
it lay for many years beneath a rank burden
of fern and scrub with, here and there,
patches of regenerated forest. It was
discovered, however, that the land was
remarkably fertile, and in the past
30 to 40 years much of it has been
transformed into highly productive grazing
land. The task has been no easy one, even
so, for this is a relatively high rainfall area
with a climate on the warm side of
temperate, in which a paddock left
ungrazed for a few weeks can rapidly revert
to a bracken-covered wilderness.

And then again, communities were born and grew up in isolation one from
another. In the South Island, communities tended to grow at the end of each road
or railway as it stretched forth from the original settlement, over plain and river and
coastal hill. In the North Island, settlers were landed by boat in little coastal
enclaves which were separated from each other by hundreds of miles of dense
forest, rugged terrain and, often, hostile tribes. They remained isolated until road
and rail pushed through to them. One of the greatest marks of man's occupation,
then, consists of engineering feats where almost insurmountable difficulties of
terrain were overcome, like the Raurimu Spiral, which is a stretch of the main trunk
railway line where the gradient of 1 in 50 was overcome by the laying of the track
in a complete circle, with three horseshoe curves and two tunnels.

There are, of course, other marks. The towns are often less well planned than
those of the South Island, largely because, in a hostile environment, settlers' houses
were huddled closely together for security and comfort. Also, the quarter-acres that
were pegged out for each family dwelling usually had to be hacked out from the
close-crowding bush; so streets, created with vast and herculean effort, are often
narrower than their South Island counterparts.

Roads, pushed through the wilderness so that soldiers could move quickly from
point to point, were only as wide as was necessary to accommodate a train of
artillery or a column of infantry, and they tended to stick close to the valley floors.
Where swamps and rivers forced the roads to climb higher, they followed the crests
of ridges at gradients practical for bullock wagons. Today, gradients have been
made easier on motorways, main trunk routes and some secondary systems, and
bends which were dangerous for modern, high-speed traffic have been eased or
straightened; but the country roads still follow the bullock and pack-horse trails,
and though usually sealed, are still frequently anachronistically narrow.

FAR LEFT: THE CITY OF AUCKLAND

Auckland, once the seat of government, has long been New Zealand's largest, most cosmopolitan city. With its tall, white high-rises in the city centre and its sprawling suburbs scrambling over a scatter of ancient volcanic cones, the city is a vital, lively, well-favoured home for around a million New Zealanders. A focal point of the ever-changing city skyline is the Sky Tower, from which adrenalin junkies can make an exhilarating 192m jump down the side of the tower – making it the highest tower-based jump in the world.

ABOVE LEFT: RANGITOTO ISLAND AND THE WAITEMATA HARBOUR

Aucklanders enjoy an outdoor lifestyle and their outdoor activities often centre on the lovely Waitemata Harbour, a Maori name which very appropriately means 'sparkling waters'. Brooding over the harbour is the symmetrical cone of Rangitoto, a 260m (853ft) volcano, extinct but of recent enough activity to be a barren place of jagged lava and scoria, and stunted, stubborn plant life. The Waitemata is also where the America's Cup yachting challenge will be sailed every four years for as long as Team New Zealand continues to retain the trophy.

BELOW LEFT: AUCKLAND HARBOUR BRIDGE

Built in 1959 and now accommodating up to 160 000 vehicles every day, Auckland's Harbour Bridge soars over the waters that separate downtown Auckland from the North Shore. Organised bridge climbs are a great way to get a true bird's eye view of the city and harbour from the top of the bridge's span.

51

BELOW: DAIRY HERD NEAR CARTERTON, WAIRARAPA

The rolling country of the northern Wairarapa gives way, in the south, to a wide and slightly undulating plain before sinking down on its western side into the depression filled by Lake Wairarapa and Lake Onoke. To the east the land rises again to terminate in high bluffs overlooking Cook Strait. This relatively flat land is fine dairying country, where dairy herds such as these Jersey cows browse in a tree-dotted lushly green landscape.

RIGHT: LANDSCAPE BETWEEN NEW PLYMOUTH AND MT TARANAKI

The land about the northern skirts of Mt Taranaki is a crumpled, steep tract, heavily forested a mere century ago, and still carrying areas of dense bush on the actual flank of the mountain and on the shattered remains of what was once Taranaki's twin volcano.

Left: the Kaukatea Valley, near Wanganui

The Kaukatea Valley still wears patches of the native bush which once covered much of this landscape. The bush has mostly been replaced with stands of poplars and conifers, but there are still cabbage trees dotting the paddocks. The cabbage tree is a member of the lily family. Its trunk is useless for building, composed as it is of tightly packed, coarse fibres; yet the pioneers found the tree valuable. The heart of its palm-like foliage can be cooked like cabbage – Captain Cook made use of it as a kind of sauerkraut, to protect his crew against scurvy – and very tender and palatable it is.

Above: the Waiau Valley, near Wairoa, Hawke's Bay

From a number of small streams flowing down from the Urewera highlands towards Lake Waikaremoana, the Waiau River is formed. It does not flow into the lake, but turns eastwards and flows down to join the Wairoa about 16km (10 miles) from the little hamlet and one-time garrison post of Frasertown. A wild stretch of water in its upper reaches, flowing through wild country, it quietens as the countryside softens, and presently drifts peaceably through a green and pleasant valley shaded with oak and elm and willow. Yet even here the forested hills are still in plain view, so the Waiau Valley makes a sort of frontier, where cultivation and imposed order meet the primeval jungle of the Urewera hills.

ABOVE: FISHING FLEET, GISBORNE

Though the bay in which Gisborne sits is called Poverty Bay, the district is a region of rich productivity. Fine wines are grown around Gisborne, and much of the countryside is highly favoured pastureland. Fishing is very much a minor industry, yet a small off-shore fishing fleet operates out of the river-mouth harbour. Near the centre of the city and only a little distance upstream from the coast, the Waimata and Taruheru Rivers join to form the Turanganui River, which is thus the shortest river in New Zealand.

RIGHT: MARAETAI DAM AND MANGAKINO

One of several hydro-electric dams on the Waikato River, the Maraetai Dam, 87m (285ft) high, has formed a lake nearly 600 hectares (1482 acres) in extent and 76m (250ft) deep. Mangakino township was established in the late 1940s for the accommodation of construction workers on the Maraetai Dam and two other hydro dams, Whakamaru and Atiamuri, upstream. When construction was complete, the township remained as a market and administrative centre for a land settlement scheme which turned the scrub and fern wastelands into highly productive farmland.

Left: Wylie Cottage, Gisborne

The pioneers in the wild areas around Poverty Bay seldom had time for the building of large houses. Nevertheless, many of the pioneer houses remaining are gems of graceful and dignified architecture, though built in a way which ensured comparative ease and speed of erection. This beautiful little house is a straightforward, uncomplicated rectangle, with a roofed veranda across the front and a lean-to extension at the rear. The upper floor is lit by windows under the gables and a small dormer. Weatherboarding timbers are laid vertically, not overlapping but with weatherproofing cleats over the joins. The roof is shingled. Overall, it is a delightful little home, still full of charm.

Below: the Treaty House, Waitangi

The official name for this house was The Residency, for it was the dwelling, office and court of the Lieutenant Governor. Designed by the official Colonial Architect, it has a Georgian cleanness and simplicity. Its rooms are well proportioned and spacious, and its French windows look out across a sweep of lawn to the Bay of Islands. On the lawn, the Treaty of Waitangi was presented and signed in 1840.

PREVIOUS PAGE: LANDSCAPE NEAR TAUMARUNUI

The King Country is a region of contrasts – of green sheep runs on ruggedly steep country, of ploughed fields and surprisingly precipitous rock faces, of sudden marches of dark forest enwrapping willow-shaded brooks in valley meadows – and Taumarunui, a bustling township deep in the King Country hills.

ABOVE: WANGANUI FROM PAPAITI HILL

Wanganui, at the mouth of the Whanganui River, was one of New Zealand's earliest settlements, and is, today, one of the country's most picturesque cities. It is renowned for its delightful public parks and gardens, for its beautiful homes and, most of all, for its river. The city possesses a number of architectural splendours and landmarks, such as the lookout tower (seen on the far horizon) on Durie Hill. An elevator ascends the side of the hill, making it easier for visitors to approach the castellated stone tower.

ABOVE: WELLINGTON CITY AT NIGHT

Wellington, the nation's capital city, is superbly situated about an immense, almost land-locked harbour, of which nineteenth-century commentators used to say that it would shelter all the navies of the world in perfect security. Often likened to San Francisco, it really has little in common with that great city, except, perhaps, that its business area and older suburbs are crowded about its waterfront, and cling to the steep slopes overlooking the harbour. The rest of the city is spread over the surrounding hills, around the sea-coast bays and in the bush-filled valleys.

LEFT: PALMERSTON NORTH

Palmerston North spreads across the Rangitikei Plain some 129km (80 miles) north of Wellington – a cross-roads from which the main routes run out to Taranaki, Hawke's Bay and Auckland. The centre of the city is built around a gorgeously gardened square, through which the railway used to run before it was banished to the northern outskirts of the city. In spring the city exhibits a glorious flowering of cherry trees.

LEFT: CENTRAL WELLINGTON

Wellington, glittering here at dusk, was quick to adopt the fashion for high-rise buildings. Chronically short of land, the early builders had to reclaim space from the harbour itself, and crowded many official buildings hard back against the harbourside cliffs. But as commercial and Government enterprises grew, even the reclaimed land could not readily accommodate them, so Wellington's centre now leaps upward in towers of steel and glass and concrete.

ABOVE: WELLINGTON FROM MT VICTORIA

Part of Wellington's downtown waterfront, viewed here from Mt Victoria, is today dominated by the massive structure that is Te Papa, the Museum of New Zealand (centre left), which opened in 1998.

ABOVE LEFT: TUGS, MT MAUNGANUI

Mt Maunganui serves as Tauranga's deep-sea port. The port, which is situated on a narrow neck of the headland forming the eastern head of Tauranga Harbour, takes its name from Mt Maunganui proper, a 252m (827ft) eminence at the end of the headland. The port serves a huge paper pulp and forestry enterprise inland from the Bay of Plenty. On the ocean coast, Mt Maunganui Beach is famous and favoured for its splendid surf.

BELOW LEFT: TAURANGA BOAT HARBOUR

Tauranga Harbour, protected from the Pacific storms by the long, low Matakana Island, is highly favoured by small-boat enthusiasts. The harbour offers some 24km (15 miles) of superb boating water, with many small inlets of almost tropical appearance with tall tree ferns leaning over the water like palm trees, and areas of mangrove.

RIGHT: LAKE ROTOROA, HAMILTON

Rotoroa means, simply, 'Long Lake'. It is a peaceful place, lying just beyond Hamilton's busy downtown centre, and has gardened shores and shady trees and a population of magnificent black swans. Houses stand back from its shores, surrounded by colourful gardens. Huge Monarch butterflies and a variety of native birds are common here – and the business-like towers of the city are just far enough beyond it all to heighten the feeling of tranquillity.

LEFT: WAIRARAPA LANDSCAPE

When Europeans first came to it, much of the Wairarapa was under heavy forest – in particular, an area known as Seventy Mile Bush. Hardy Scandinavian pioneers arrived in the district, in which they had been allotted land, and first had to become lumberjacks, felling the tall timber trees, clearing the forest and then building their small communities wherever they managed to clear space to accommodate them. As the timber was cut out, they returned to their original purpose and became farmers, establishing in these fertile valleys and on these rugged hills the farms which, today, are some of the most highly productive in the land.

ABOVE: TRELAWNEY STUD, NEAR CAMBRIDGE

In the Waikato, racehorses are bred on the rolling, gentle hills. The soft climate gives them year-round free-range grazing, one of the secrets of their remarkable stamina; and on the training tracks in this lovely countryside, many a racecourse legend has had its beginnings. Yet the first association between this country and the horse had little to do with racing. Its first horses were

almost certainly troopers' mounts, for this peaceful, rather English-looking countryside was once a wild military frontier between the Waikato and the King Country.

OVER PAGE: THE WAIAU VALLEY, NEAR WAIROA, HAWKE'S BAY

For all its quiet, its pastoral peace, its willows and poplars and orderly fields, the Waiau Valley is almost at the extreme edge of European man's conquest of the land. Just a little farther on, the Urewera highlands rise up, wild and forested and unforgiving, the homeland of the Tuhoe people.

The Shape of the Shore

THERE is, at the very northern tip of the North Island, a most dramatic meeting of the Pacific Ocean and the Tasman Sea. Eastwards and westwards, they seem to have their own shades of blue and turquoise green, colours which change so subtly as the eye moves towards the meeting place of their waters that it would be impossible to tell where the one ceases and the other begins, were it not for the foam and fury, the eddy and chop where their currents clash.

From that point on, down both coasts of the North Island, there is a general similarity. The west coast begins with the long, smooth sweep of Ninety Mile Beach, but soon breaks into a series of inlets and harbours – the Hokianga, which winds it way past huge sand dunes and penetrates a hilly landscape of farms and forest; the Kaipara, huge and many-branched, its inlets dotted with hamlet and township which, before adequate roads were pushed through, were served by a passenger ferry and cargo scows; the Manukau, shallow and broad; the Waikato river-mouth; Raglan and Kawhia. And then begins a series of beaches which run in sweeping curves to the rock-bound shores of the North Taranaki Bight. High cliffs overhang black iron sands, which give gradually to the golden sands of the South Taranaki Bight shores. The coastline runs in a single, sweeping curve southwards to Waikanae, Paraparaumu and Raumati and then becomes reef-bound as it runs past Paekakariki. The long Tasman swell, rolling in between the islands of Kapiti and Mana, crashes over the jagged rocks to the very base of the high bluffs. The road creeps past along a rocky ledge barely above the sea, before swinging inland, over the hills to Wellington. But the shoreline swings around cliff and headland, past the shallow harbour of Porirua and the long inlet that runs into Pauatahanui. It runs down beneath the lofty hills of Makara and around Cape Terawhiti, along the Cook Strait shore to the magnificent Wellington harbour.

The east coast, immediately south of North Cape, is broken and deeply indented with mangrove-fringed harbours – Parengarenga, Rangaunu Bay and the perfect horseshoe shape of Doubtless Bay. Past that again, there is Whangaroa Harbour, long and zig-zagging, and then the fascinating Bay of Islands. Further south, the shore is notched by Whangaruru Harbour and the

PIHA, AUCKLAND

West coast beaches, by and large, seem wilder than those on the east coast. Piha, west of Auckland, is a favoured holiday resort which possesses a wild grandeur that makes holiday baches, bright swimsuits and the dark heads that bob in the mighty surf all but unnoticeable. Lion Rock (so named because it resembles a lion couchant), the Piha Stream sweeping into the sea by the lion's tail, and the bush-clad headlands combine in a spectacular seascape on which man has managed to make very little impression.

ABOVE: WHANARUA BAY, BAY OF PLENTY

Where the Bay of Plenty coastline heads north-eastward towards East Cape, it takes a sudden turn due east between Waikawa Point and Otiki Point, and there are 12 or 13km (7 or 8 miles) of small northward-facing bays. These tree-fringed, reef-bound bays include many delightfully sheltered little coves such as Whanarua Bay, highly favoured by holiday-makers.

RIGHT: KAWA KAWA BAY, EAST CAPE

North of East Cape, and immediately south of Hicks Bay, Kawa Kawa Bay is typical of the East Cape coves, with its sandy beach and its wave-carved reefs, lying isolated and lonely beneath frowning, bush-clad cliffs. Here, in December, the pohutukawa blazes scarlet along the coastline, and the Pacific Ocean pounds in towards the steep, high land. Crayfish are caught here – the enormous Packhorse variety.

almost completely land-locked, splendidly sheltered Whangarei Harbour. Then comes the magnificent sweep of Bream Bay and the broad, island-dotted Hauraki Gulf, which takes in the ragged Mahurangi and Whangaparaoa Peninsulas before the coastline leads down to Auckland's Waitemata Harbour. Eastwards from the Gulf, across the Coromandel Peninsula, the Bay of Plenty presents some 320km (200 miles) of coastline, much of it in long curves of golden sand, broken by the southward curving inlet of Mercury Bay, a number of smaller, narrower inlets, Tauranga Harbour and Ohiwa Harbour, before curving north-eastward to Cape Runaway. South of East Cape, the Pacific Ocean beats into a long succession of small, sandy, reef-girt beaches, gouges out a deep curve at Poverty Bay and takes a 160km (100 mile) bite into the land at Hawke Bay. From Cape Kidnappers, it runs southward along sandy, reef-protected beaches and open stretches of mighty surf, with the high, steep hills rising up almost from the water's edge, until it turns westward around Cape Palliser and the wide scoop of Palliser Bay, rounds Turakirae Head and Pencarrow Head, and enters the Wellington harbour.

Both coasts possess an abundance of inlets and harbours, making them a small-boat skipper's paradise, though the weather and the boisterousness of the sea along the western side of the island can be daunting. Both, but particularly the east coast, show a remarkable variety of scenery, from the sub-tropical, mangrove-bordered harbours of Northland to the surf-pounded gravel beaches and severe cliffs along the edge of Cook Strait. There are beaches protected by bush-crowned headlands, including Hot Water Beach, where hot water seeps through the sands and for as long as anyone can remember, both locals and tourists have bathed luxuriously, scooping hollows in the wet sand at low tide. There are bays dotted with islets, and as many crayfish to be found as on the South Island's Kaikoura coast. There are, perhaps, fewer beaches rendered unsafe

LEFT: WESTERN COAST OF COROMANDEL PENINSULA FROM KIRITA HILL

Kirita Hill is a 394m (1293ft) rise overlooking Manaia Harbour and Kirita Bay which affords a superlative view of the Hauraki Gulf. The islands just offshore are Wekarua and Rangipukea. Wekarua means 'nest of the woodhen', which suggests that the pre-European Maori found the offshore islets rich storehouses of edible bird life, making this idyllic region a place where the living was easy.

ABOVE RIGHT: MATAURI BAY, NORTHLAND

Sheltered by a lofty headland, Matauri Bay is a glorious 1.5km (1 mile) stretch of golden sand, a little to the south-east of Whangaroa Harbour, on Northland's east coast. Commercial fishing is carried on in the bay, and 5 or 6km (3 or 4 miles) offshore lie the famed Cavalli Islands, a favoured big-game fishing ground. Matauri Bay serves as a base for big-game fishing launches.

BELOW RIGHT: LONELY COVE, COROMANDEL PENINSULA

Lonely Cove is a short, broad sweep of golden sand, backed by tall limestone cliffs and a pleasant, pohutukawa-shaded grassy strip. The cove is separated from the grander and more frequented sweep of Cooks Beach by a tree-crowned headland. Its northern end is dominated by a tall bluff on which stands the Captain James Cook Memorial, commemorating Cook's visit to the area. As the monument's inscription says, 'In this bay was anchored 5–15 November, 1796, HMS Endeavour, Lieutenant James Cook, Commander. He observed the Transit of Mercury and named this Bay.' The bay is named, of course, Mercury Bay, on which Lonely Cove is a minor indentation.

OVER PAGE: MERCURY BAY, COROMANDEL PENINSULA

Mercury Bay is almost triangular, and is lined with lesser bays and inlets and glorious sweeps of sandy beach. Here, on 4 November 1769, Cook wrote in his journal: 'My reasons for putting in here were the hopes of discovering a good harbour and the disire I had of being in some convenient place to observe the transit of Mercury ... If we should be so fortunate as to obtain this Observation the Longitude of this place and Country will thereby be very accurately determined.'

LEFT: HOKIANGA HARBOUR

The Hokianga Harbour winds and twists
deep inland, past Opononi and Omapere.
Long, narrow inlets reach up between
scrub-patched hills. This is the scene of
some of the earliest European history in
New Zealand, and is the vicinity in which
Baron de Thierry tried to set up an
independent kingdom. The harbour mouth
is guarded by great, tawny sandhills, and its
shores are dotted with small, picturesque
villages, such as Rawene and Kohukohu.
The harbour itself is shallow.

ABOVE: MATAI BAY, NORTHLAND

The northern end of Doubtless Bay is a
rectangular peninsula, the northern
extremity of which is Cape Karikari. At the
base of this cape, a horseshoe curve of
white beach backed by rolling, timber-
patched country provides a small-boat
anchorage which is almost land-locked. It is
an idyllic little retreat with patches of
cabbage trees, tree ferns and nikau palms
to give it a tropical look.

ABOVE: TAUPO BAY AND WHANGAROA HARBOUR, NORTHLAND

The little, clean, dazzling stretch of sand that marks Taupo Bay is lined with cottages and homes which look out across the blue water to Stephenson Island. The beach terminates in the steep and rocky face of the range of hills separating it from the splendidly land-locked Whangaroa Harbour, with its entrance guarded by fantastic rock walls. Whangaroa was once a loading port for kauri timber. In 1890 the ship Boyd called here and was attacked and burned by the Maori in revenge for the flogging of the son of a chief, who had served aboard the ship.

RIGHT: TONGAPORUTU, TARANAKI

Where the Tongaporutu River flows out into the North Taranaki Bight, some 56km (35 miles) north of New Plymouth, stand great sandstone cliffs, riddled with caverns by the actions of the restless Tasman Sea. Just off the southern head, at the river's mouth, is a sort of Maori Gibraltar, a castle-like rock which was held against attack until 1821 by Ngati Tama warriors. In that year, the remnant of defenders abandoned it. The Tongaporutu River is navigable by launch for a distance of some 16km (10 miles) from its mouth, and is famed for its glorious scenery.

by tidal rip and in-shore current than is the case in the South Island – probably because the North Island's coastline is so much more irregular, with jutting headlands and major capes foiling the ocean currents, diverting them as a granite cliff diverts the most powerful river.

Because of the character of the New Zealand coast, European New Zealanders became seafarers from the earliest days of settlement. Communication between the coast-hugging little pioneer settlements was easier by sea than by land, and coastal shipping carried the bulk of the country's early trade. Oddly, though, the Maori, whose ancestors came to New Zealand by feats of magnificent seamanship, largely deserted the ocean once they became settled, confining their navigation to river and lake, taking to the sea only for off-shore fishing.

Naturally, the earliest European settlements were built close to the sea. The whalers, of course, planted their rumbustious bases in sheltered bays and coves, and the people who came to New Zealand in organised settlement schemes built their homes close to the shores on which they landed. The largest cities and towns, therefore, are either on the coast or on rivers which are, or once were, navigable. Most New Zealanders become joyously familiar with the white Pacific surf or the moody Tasman early in life, and look with pity upon those less favoured peoples whose beaches are fenced and swept and overwhelmingly crowded. It is the ambition of many New Zealanders to retire somewhere near the sea, because the coast offers interest and recreation for people long after they have ceased taking an active part in mountain pursuits and other vigorous pastimes; and anyway, from the coast it is usually possible to look inland and see, on the far horizon, a pride of rugged peaks, especially from the west coast beaches. And that, of course, is possessing the best of both worlds.

ABOVE: CAPE KIDNAPPERS, HAWKE'S BAY

This sharp-edged ridge, which droops down like a dragon's tail ending in island spikes of rock, marks the southern extremity of Hawke Bay. .(Oddly, the province is Hawke's Bay and the bay itself is Hawke Bay.) On the crest of the ridge, on two flat platforms devoid of vegetation, gannet colonies are to be found. The gannet is a relative of the pelican. It rarely nests on mainland sites, usually choosing small, steep-sided offshore islands.

84

LEFT: STATUE OF CAPTAIN COOK, GISBORNE

The visit of Captain Cook to Poverty Bay was not a particularly happy one, for he found the Maori here unwilling to trade fresh provisions and even reluctant to allow him to replenish his fresh water supply. This was in complete contrast to the treatment he had received to the north, where the open-handedness of the inhabitants caused him to name the region Bay of Plenty. Behind this statue, which stands on Gisborne's foreshore, is the distant headland he called Young Nick's Head, after a cabin boy, Nicholas Young, who first sighted it.

ABOVE: TONGUE POINT, WELLINGTON

Tongue Point, with its narrow, shingly beach walled by steep bluffs and high hills, juts out into Cook Strait about 6.5km (4 miles) south-east of Cape Terawhiti and 12km (7 1/2 miles) west of the entrance to Wellington Harbour. The hills of Marlborough in the South Island may be seen from Tongue Point, slightly hazy with distance, rising up across 40km (25 miles) of somewhat turbulent sea. The point, with its isolated spread of green pasture, is often buffeted by the Cook Strait gales.

BELOW: URQUHARTS BAY, WHANGAREI

Where the Pacific flows into Whangarei Harbour, it swirls around Marsden Point, gouging out a broad curve on the opposite shore which is called Urquharts Bay. Over the bay stands a 420m (1378ft) peak known as Manaia, named after a legendary Maori chieftain who sent his principal fighting chief off to battle distant enemies, then stole his wife. The outraged husband returned and attacked Manaia's pa, and chased Manaia, his two children and his faithless wife. Before he could kill them, the gods turned them all into stone, and there they can be seen to this day, pillars of rock on top of the bluff.

RIGHT: ANAURA BAY, EAST COAST

The bush is gone, replaced by sheep and cattle, and the whares on the hillsides have been supplanted by small houses here and there, but Captain Cook would still recognise the cove he visited in 1769. He came ashore with a watering party and sat on the hillside above the bay to make a sketch of the sailors filling barrels, and of Pourewa Island, which he called Sporing Island after the assistant naturalist. He would find, today, a small marker on a plateau overlooking the lovely beach, relating how he got wood and water, and Joseph Banks and Daniel Solander collected plants, that day in October 1769.

ABOVE: KIRITA BAY, COROMANDEL
PENINSULA

Below Kirita Hill and opening into the
Hauraki Gulf, Kirita Bay looks out across the
mouth of the Firth of Thames, to the
ancient volcanic humps which rise up south
of Auckland, 26km (16 miles) across the
calm Hauraki waters. The whole of the
peninsula's western coast is notched with
such calm and sheltered coves.

RIGHT: PIERCY ROCK, BAY OF ISLANDS

The eastern headland of the entrance to the
Bay of Islands is a slim finger of land called
Cape Brett. Some little distance offshore,
looking like a piece of the cape which has
been broken off and tossed carelessly into
the water, stands Piercy Island, better
known to thousands of tourists and
fishermen as The Hole in the Rock. The
cavern which pierces the sharp-topped
pinnacle is lofty enough to allow pleasure
launches to sail through it.

Left: Te Araroa

Spread along the curve of a bay between Hicks Bay and East Cape, Te Araroa lies beneath a lofty, scarred bluff. It is a favourite holiday spot, with its sandy beaches and occasional reefs along its shoreline. Te Araroa possesses an enormous, venerable pohutukawa tree, claimed to be the largest in New Zealand and possibly the oldest.

Above Right: East Cape and Pohutukawa Tree

On this eastern-most finger of land, beyond which there is nothing but empty ocean for thousands of miles, the hills are eroded and gaunt. The salt-laden sea winds whip along the beaches, bending the gnarled, tough pohutukawa trees and scorching the grasses. This country is sheep country. The inhabitants are still predominantly Maori, enjoying a life-style which contains strong links with the land and with Maori tradition.

Below Right: Pohutukawa Blossoms

For all that it clings to rocky coastal cliffs and wind-parched, battered shores, the pohutukawa, gnarled and twisted, still produces a Christmas-time blaze of scarlet blooms year after year. There is a legend that when the first Maori arrived in New Zealand, they saw pohutukawa blossoms along the shores and promptly threw away the prized but faded red ceremonial feathers they had brought from their tropical homeland and gathered the blossoms instead, only to find that they faded and fell apart very quickly. Today the blossoms are under threat from the possum, a marsupial with an appetite for the green leaves, young buds and shoots of the pohutukawa.

LEFT: BAY OF ISLANDS, FROM RAWHITI

Rawhiti is a scattered farming community on the long writhing tail of land that terminates at Cape Brett. From its hilltops there is a magnificent panoramic view westward and northward to the Bay of Islands. Urupukapuka and several smaller islands sprawl offshore, across the Albert Channel, and in an inlet on the island's southern side is the big-game fishing base known as Zane Grey's Camp.

ABOVE: RUSSELL, BAY OF ISLANDS

The peaceful and rather quaint little town of Russell was once Kororareka, easy winner of the title 'Hell-Hole of the Pacific'. It was a base for whalers, sealers, traders and all the sweepings of the sea. Noisy with grog shops, it was eventually burned to the ground by angry Maori. Only the Anglican Christ Church, which is still scarred with bullet holes, and Bishop Pompallier's house remain. Both buildings were respected as mission property, and spared by the Maori.

LEFT: WAINUI BAY, NORTHLAND

Between Whangaroa Harbour and Matauri
Bay, where the hills come down to the
Pacific, is Wainui Bay – another of
Northland's delightful sweeps of clean
yellow sand. Wainui Bay is one of New
Zealand's lesser known holiday resorts. With
its occasional rocky reefs, its gently shelving
shore, its grassy headlands and its
pohutukawa, it lies at the end of a twisting,
somewhat steep hill road from Whangaroa.

ABOVE: MATAI BAY, NORTHLAND

The small headland that juts into the blue
waters of Matai Bay is tipped with a broken
outcropping of rock, forming rock pools
which are alive with shellfish, starfish and
the myriad forms of tidal marine life.

LEFT: GANNET COLONY, CAPE KIDNAPPERS

The gannets that nest on the dragon-tail promontory of Cape Kidnappers are the Australian gannet, large white birds with yellow heads and black wing-tips. They feed on small fish, and nest from November through December. This gannet rookery is believed to be the only mainland rookery in the world. Usually the birds nest on small, rocky, offshore islands.

ABOVE RIGHT: KARIKARI BAY, NORTHLAND

On the northern side of the peninsula which encloses Doubtless Bay, Karikari Bay lies open to the Pacific Ocean. The country behind it is comparatively low-lying, with sand dunes and, dramatic in its shape and its sudden elevation, an ancient volcanic cone at the western end of the beach.

BELOW RIGHT: CASTLEPOINT LIGHTHOUSE, WAIRARAPA COAST

The fine, sandy, gently shelving beach at Castlepoint terminates dramatically in an upward-sloping reef, spreading below a rocky bluff with the limestone pinnacles that give the place its name. A stretch of the reef is like a man-made sea wall, enclosing a small lagoon. At its northern end, the reef thrusts out into deep water, lifting a slender spire of lighthouse at its tip, like an exclamation point, drawing attention to the fact that here, for coastal vessels, is danger.

LEFT: MT MAUNGANUI BEACH

From the foot of Maunganui, ancient fortress-hill, the beach curves southward, fronting the low-lying isthmus which forms the southern 'breakwater' of Tauranga's harbour. Once the scene of bloody battles, this beach is now one of New Zealand's best-known and most favoured holiday resorts, especially popular with surfers.

ABOVE: YACHT HARBOUR AND MT VICTORIA, WELLINGTON

Tucked in between the Overseas Passenger Terminal and the sandy stretch of beach at Oriental Bay, the Wellington Yacht Harbour is a still, calm haven on which colourful pleasure-craft bob gently at moorings, like waterlilies on a pond. The hillside suburb of Roseneath climbs the northern and western slopes of Mt Victoria, the houses clustered about the old convent like a medieval village about its castle.

ABOVE: CAPE REINGA, NORTHLAND

Cape Reinga is almost the northernmost part of New Zealand. It plays an important part in Maori lore, as the departing place of the spirits of the dead. It juts out to form the western extremity of Spirits Bay, and the Tasman Sea and the Pacific Ocean meet at its tip in a fury of conflicting currents.

RIGHT: MAKARORI BEACH, EAST CAPE

Makarori Beach is one of several East Cape seaside resorts just north of Gisborne. The warm climate and open sandy beaches, sometimes shaded by huge pohutukawa trees, ensure that Makarori, Wainui and similar adjacent resorts are well populated during summer months.

South Island

A Perfection of Grandeur

FIRST-TIME visitors to New Zealand, describing their impressions, might well say, simply, 'The country is mountainous.' It wouldn't be telling the full tale, but such a description would convey a fairly adequate picture. New Zealand is mountainous; and even in those areas where it is not, its plains, coastlines, lakes, cities and rolling pastoral landscapes are brooded over, dominated by mountains. Where the eye looks inland, it is usually guided on and upwards to a high, serrated skyline, sometimes dark with forest to the crests of notched ridges, sometimes dazzling with year-round snow. Single summits, or prides of powerful peaks, mountains are the predominant feature, the key component which establishes the character of the entire scene.

This, in varying degrees, is true of both North and South Islands. But it is in the South Island that the mountains reach a perfection of grandeur. The South Island is more spectacularly creased than the North Island. Viewed from almost any internal airline flight, vast areas of the South Island are seen to be as crumpled as a discarded piece of paper, with range upon range of titanic pressure-fold ridges stretching away as far as the eye can see. The Tasman Mountains, the Richmond Range, the St Arnaud and Spenser Mountains and the Kaikoura Ranges fan out northward from the great rugged chain which forms the Southern Alps. At their southern end the Alps fray out into a wild and well-nigh impenetrable tangle of mountains covering perhaps half of the Otago-Southland region.

The Southern Alps, of course, take pride of place. They are the show-piece, the magnificent spectacle, that attracts visitors in their awed thousands. In their folds they hold lakes of unrivalled splendour. On their valley-riven flanks, between their massive lateral arms, they cradle splendid glaciers. In this massif alone there are more than 130 peaks that rise over 2400 metres (7872ft), chief of which is Aoraki, the Cloud-Piercer, officially and prosaically named Aoraki/Mt Cook (after the great eighteenth-century navigator) by official and prosaic Captain Stokes of the survey ship *Acheron*, in the mid-nineteenth century.

It is the mountains, of course, that order the country's climate. The South Island is exactly what its name describes, a southern ocean island, with an island's capricious weather patterns. That is to be expected. What is astonishing, however, is the number of climatic variations, distinct climatic zones, within such a small compass; for the island is a mere 750km (465 miles) long by 250km (155 miles) wide at its widest point. And that – by continental terms – is a small area in which

LEFT: SNOWFALL, CRAIGIEBURN RANGE, CANTERBURY

The Craigieburn Range, high above Lake Lyndon on the road to Arthur's Pass, is a drab area in summer, more like a gigantic gravel heap than an alpine spur. But in winter, when the snow is down into the valleys, it is at once majestic and magical, like everyone's dream of Switzerland.

A true alpine lake, Lake Tekapo was once an ancient glacier, a prehistoric ice-burden which the surrounding countryside has never quite forgotten or forgiven. Near the lake edge, feathery snowgrass, foxglove and the spiny matagouri seem to be the only plants willing to inhabit the thin soil covering the ancient moraine.

RIGHT: GLENDHU BAY, LAKE WANAKA

Though the autumn days are warm, the shingly beach of Glendhu Bay is deserted by evening, when the last rays of the lowering sun are defeated by the early evening chill. The cold comes creeping across the deep waters of Lake Wanaka which, it is suddenly easy to recall, was once a mass of glacier ice, thousands of metres thick.

to have, side-by-side, zones which are: temperature in climate, with a moderate to low rainfall; areas which are dry to the point of being near-desert; areas of immoderately high rainfall and lush forest of almost sub-tropical luxuriance; areas which experience each winter a heavy and sustained snowfall; areas of crackling frosts; and areas with an enviable tally of annual sunshine hours.

The moisture-laden winds from the Tasman Sea bring clouds which are literally trapped on the western side of the Southern Alps, and are forced to such altitudes that they unload heavy rains onto the narrow coastal strip on the mountains' western side. The north-west winds, buffeting their way through mountain valleys as though gigantic wind-tunnels, burst upon the eastern plains with great and sometimes destructive force. The eternal snows upon those prodigious peaks refrigerate the winter air, so that east-coast towns, cities and farmlands receive crisp frosts on clear nights from late March till late September.

No South Islander lives more than two or three hours' drive from ski-slopes, ice-bound skating ponds and lakes and hillsides that are snowy from July to October. Few have not at least a nodding acquaintance with the high country, and some memorable experiences of the great ranges. At the very least, they will have memories of some mountain mood or spectacle, such as the first rays of the morning sun touching Mt Cook's summit with flame while the land is still dark, or the reflected brightness of the moonlight on the snow-clad face of the Remarkables, or the snow-covered peaks of the Kaikouras seeming to lean over the calm bay. No matter where South Islanders live – on the broad, billiard-table-flat plains of Canterbury, the rolling hills of North Otago, the rock-bound Kaikoura coast, the high uplands of the Mackenzie Country, the rock-ribbed glacier-planed terraces of Central Otago, or in the bustling towns and cities – every South Islander is, in some special way, a child of the mountains.

ABOVE LEFT: MT TALBOT, FIORDLAND

As you drive across Lyttles Flat, where the Homer Tunnel construction village once stood, and which is now fragrant with fern and mountain gentian, Mt Talbot, 2117m (6945ft), stands before you, its twisted peak retaining pockets of snow all year round. Part of the Barrier Range, a spur of the Darran mountain complex, the forbidding peak leans back from huge fans of avalanche rock.

BELOW LEFT: AILSA MOUNTAINS, HOLLYFORD VALLEY, FIORDLAND

From where the Milford Road runs through the Hollyford Valley, the Ailsa Mountains trend away south-eastward, walling off that jungle-like, beautiful wilderness from the Upper Greenstone Valley. Some of the finest tramping trails in the world wander through these primeval fastnesses.

RIGHT: GLENDHU BAY, LAKE WANAKA

A pleasant curve of beach, lined with willow and pine and adding a touch of gentleness to the bulbous, rocky faces of Glendhu Bluff and the stern mountain surrounds, Glendhu Bay is popular with swimmers in the burning summer heat. In autumn it becomes a favourite haunt of anglers, fishing for brown and rainbow trout and Atlantic salmon.

LEFT: BOWEN FALLS, MILFORD SOUNDS

Bowen Falls issue from a hanging valley high above the head of Milford Sound. The water plunges first onto an inclined, hollow rock 'springboard', from which it leaps out again in a sparkling white arc, to fall into a spray-clouded basin. The leap is most dramatic after rain; but even when the water is draped over the rocky faces of the gash in the forested mountain wall, it is hardly less beautiful.

BELOW: LAKE IANTHE, WESTLAND

Set in a scenic reserve about 15km (9 miles) from Harihari, this delightful little gem of a lake was named, it is said, by a surveyor-explorer who admired Byron's 'Childe Harold's Pilgrimage', which was dedicated to a little girl named Ianthe. If that seems to be a roundabout way of arriving at a name, perhaps it was just that the little lake's exquisite smallness (5.6 square km/2 square miles), by its very contrast with the grandeur of the mountains, brought to mind simple and charming things.

FAR LEFT: CLINTON CANYON, MILFORD TRACK

Part of the famous Milford Track winds beside the Clinton River for 23km (14 miles) through the mountain-walled valley known as the Clinton Canyon. The forested mountains rise straight up from the valley floor for perhaps 1200m (3940ft), then lean back as they stab skyward with spear-point peaks to some 1800m (6000ft) above sea level. The canyon climbs, eventually, to Mackinnon Pass, reaching up through moss-hung, twisted mountain beeches to an open area of ranunculus and mountain daisies, where keas come close, unafraid and friendly.

LEFT: FOX GLACIER

Fox Glacier's somewhat zig-zagging course brings the great ice-river down from the neve, the vast snowfields in their inclined basin between the Fritz and Fox Ranges, to a landscape of spurs covered with forest of almost tropical luxuriance. From the glacier's terminal face issues the Fox River, bursting out from an ice cave, carrying great chunks of ice as it hurries down to join the Cook River.

ABOVE: THE OKURU RIVER AND SOUTH WESTLAND MOUNTAINS

From Okuru, south of Haast, the great forested humps of hill stand up above bush and swamp to form outriders of Mt Aspiring National Park, southern extremity of the Alps proper. This is untouched country – the snow-fed river, swelled by many a tributary creek, slides across the coastal flats, flanked by sedges and flax, with a backing of shrubs, which in turn give way to tall forest trees.

ABOVE: HIGH-COUNTRY ROAD NEAR GLENMORE STATION, MACKENZIE COUNTRY

Towards the head of Lake Tekapo, the Godley Peaks rise up from the Mackenzie Country landscape of brown snowgrass and tussock, and the shelter belts of dark, hardy pines. The peaks are snow-covered in winter, but in summer are eroded and barren, like gigantic heaps of gravel, crumbling slowly to choke the Canterbury rivers and build up the vast gravel flats of the Mackenzie Basin.

RIGHT: SHOTOVER RIVER AT ARTHUR'S POINT, CENTRAL OTAGO

All the fascinating contradictions of the Central Otago landscape show in the Shotover River's writhing valley, near Queenstown. Here are the typical rock-ribbed hills, furred with brown, sun-scorched grasses and patched with matagouri and tough briars. Here are the poplars and willows, autumn-yellow from the first frosts; and amidst the harshness there is, here and there, the lush green of a cultivated field. But always, winding across the scene, are the Central Otago rivers, depositing their frequently gold-bearing gravels at the feet of rocky, broom-clad spurs.

Above: Lake Te Anau

Biggest of the South Island's lakes is Te Anau, its western shores towered over by the densely forested Murchison Mountains, its eastern side gentle with willow and bluegum where an easy, rolling countryside comes down to its shore. In the dark mountains, in 1948, two fascinating discoveries were made. By a small tarn, high in the mountains, tracks led to the finding of a bird long thought to be extinct, the colourful takahe; and near the lake's shore, almost directly beneath the tarn, the legendary and long-forgotten Te Ana-Au Caves were uncovered, with their glow-worm displays rivalling those of Waitomo.

Right: Lake Quill and Sutherland Falls

Cupped in the mountains of the Milford Sound district, Lake Quill pours a steady stream of water from a jug-like lip, to form Sutherland Falls, highest in New Zealand and third highest in the world. The first leap of the falls is a lofty 288m (945ft), the second 229m (751ft) and the third 103m (338ft). The Sutherland Falls are one of the principal attractions along the world-famous Milford Track. When Lake Quill is in flood, the Sutherland Falls curve out in a single, spectacular leap of 580m (1904ft).

ABOVE: LAKES TEKAPO AND ALEXANDRINA, FROM MT JOHN

The Mackenzie Country lakes are of two kinds – snow-fed and rain-fed. Snow-fed lakes, like Tekapo, are a beautiful lapis-lazuli blue, and rain-water lakes, like Lake Alexandrina, are green-glass clear. The Mackenzie Basin, a region named after the Scottish highland shepherd who discovered it (and tried to stock it with stolen sheep), is a wild expanse of tussock and snowgrass and clear mountain air. An observatory has been set on Mt John, to take advantage of the clear, dry atmosphere.

117

LEFT: FOX GLACIER FROM CLEARWATER FLAT

The Clearwater River rattles over stony shallows along the edge of a typical Westland river flat, which it shares with the Cook River. Its waters reflect the almost theatrical spectacle of clouds slowly parting like stage curtains to reveal, first the Fox Glacier in its notch in the granite mountains, and then the splendour of the stupendous peaks from which the glacier flows.

BELOW: MT TASMAN, FROM FOX, SOUTH WESTLAND

The peaks of the Southern Alps are never more spectacular, never more clearly, magnificently displayed, than they are from South Westland, that narrow coastal shelf at their very feet. Mt Tasman, 3498m (11 475ft), cradles on its faces the snows which feed the Balfour and Abel Janzoon Glaciers, the latter spilling down into the vast neve which gives birth to the mighty Fox Glacier.

ABOVE: AORAKI/MT COOK AND SEALY TARN

Aoraki/Mt Cook, the Cloud-Piercer, New Zealand's highest mountain, with the long chain of peaks trailing southward to form an impressive wall on the eastern side of the Hooker Glacier, is awe-inspiring country. From Sealy Tarn little can be seen of the Hooker Glacier except the long heaping of gravel and boulders which it has left behind in its retreat back into the high reaches beneath Turner Peak and Proud Pass. But in mountain meadows such as this grow the famed Mount Cook lily (upper right) and the mountain daisy (lower right) which, in season, are a sight worth seeing.

OVER: LAKE MATHESON, WESTLAND

Lake Matheson, near Fox Glacier in South Westland, is a more familiar sight to many New Zealanders and visitors than far bigger lakes – because the quality of its mountain reflections makes this bush-fringed lake a favourite photographic subject. It was once a huge block of ice, left behind in ancient times by the receding glacier, and the forest which crowds down to its brim grows over a moraine which was left behind, marking a stage in the glacier's early growth, before it began its long retreat.

LEFT: WESTLAND BUSH AND STREAM

On the western side of the ranges, where the rainfall is frequent and heavy, the bush has an almost tropical luxuriance. Living trees are coated, furred, festooned with parasitic growth. Dead forest giants lie on the forest floor, crumbling beneath a burden of fungi and mosses. An unbelievable variety of ferns peer from flying-buttress root systems of trees, or reach for the sky on rough, palm-like trunks. Strange and riotous growth clothes mossy banks and droops from host trees; and the whole struggling growth fights upward, competing for a share of sunshine.

BELOW: LAKE BRUNNER FROM LONE TREE LOOKOUT, WESTLAND

When they found it in its high setting of forested foothills, Europeans named it Lake Brunner. The Maori, perhaps more alive to the poetry of its calm beauty, had long before named it Moana Kotuku, the Sea of the White Heron. Whatever it is called, the beautiful water is a vista of calm loveliness. It spreads across 26 square km (10 square miles) and is the largest of all the Westland lakes. It is constantly replenished by the run-off of Westland's heavy and frequent rains in the surrounding mountains.

OVER ABOVE: SHEEP MUSTERING BENEATH AORAKI/MT COOK, MACKENZIE COUNTRY

In the Canterbury high country, Merino sheep graze all through summer on the sparse, sun-ripened grasses, foraging over the tops of hills which, in another country, would be listed among the high mountains. But Aoraki/Mt Cook, snow-covered even in high summer, and the central massif of the Southern Alps gaze down upon the dun-coloured pastures, and their snows chill the breath of the westerly winds.

FAR RIGHT: MT ASPIRING, SOUTHERN ALPS

The great spire of Mt Aspiring soars 3027m
(9929ft) into the sky, towering above the
surrounding peaks of Stargazer, Mt Joffre,
Mt French, Moonraker and Mt Avalanche.
It is a great white fang of a peak after which
is named the Mt Aspiring National Park, a
wilderness of eternally snow-covered tops
and deep, densely forested valleys
spreading over an immense 287 205
hectares (709 396 acres).

RIGHT: SKI-PLANE ON TASMAN GLACIER

The Tasman Glacier, sweeping down like a
gleaming 29km (18 mile) staircase from
beneath the peak of Mt Elie de Beaumont
to the gravelly valley of the Tasman River,
may be climbed. But it is more easily, more
spectacularly mounted in a ski-plane, which
flies its passengers around the mighty
peaks, and lands them on the glacier's neve,
a matchlessly thrilling experience.

ABOVE: THE LIGHTHOUSE, SKIPPERS ROAD, QUEENSTOWN

The famous – or infamous – road that wanders and climbs precariously through Skippers Canyon leads into a harsh landscape, where the rocky frame of the mountains bursts out through the thin, parched soil, and rock formations have inspired fanciful names, like the Lighthouse. Perhaps the gold-fossickers found it comforting, in this unforgiving land, to imagine that such features might have been raised by men's hands rather than rudely sculpted, as they were, by climatic severity.

ABOVE RIGHT: REMARKABLES LANDSCAPE, NEAR QUEENSTOWN

As if relenting briefly, Central Otago now and again produces scenes of pastoral peace, such as these green and pleasant fields at the foot of the stern Remarkables Range – pockets of sun-trapped fertility amid the rugged mountains. The Remarkables, with peaks over 2000m (6560ft) high, and harsh, seamed faces, loom over Lake Wakatipu and make the soft pastures seem even more gentle by comparison. But even in these grassy fields, the hardy Merino and Corriedale do best, thriving where other breeds would succumb to the fierce alpine climate.

BELOW RIGHT: LAKE ALEXANDRINA, MACKENZIE COUNTRY

Lake Alexandrina, close to Lake Tekapo, forms a soft and comfortable oasis in the quilted landscape of brown hills. Even the water looks different from that of its neighbour, for this lake is rain-fed, not snow-fed. From the air, the contrasting colours of the snow-fed and rain-fed lakes of the Mackenzie Basin give an impression of jewels in a golden setting.

ABOVE: SKIPPERS BRIDGE AND THE UPPER
SHOTOVER RIVER

In the 1860s, into the dark and forbidding
mountain country came thousands of gold-
seekers; and the Shotover River rewarded
many of them richly. From others it
withheld its wealth, and yet others it
drowned, trapping them in its sudden
floods, in deep and rocky gorges. In this
kind of country man's engineering appears
frail and spidery beside the imposing
landscape of rock and crag.

LEFT: FRANKTON ARM, LAKE WAKATIPU,
AND THE REMARKABLES

The Frankton Arm of Lake Wakatipu pokes
eastward from the main body of the lake,
running beneath the rugged faces of the
Remarkables Range, lapping the shore of
the peninsula at Queenstown and the pine-
covered tip of Kelvin Heights peninsula. The
township of Frankton spreads itself down to
the water's edge, where the lake waters
gather for a turbulent rush through the
Kawarau Gorge.

131

ABOVE: TASMAN GLACIER SKI-FIELD, SOUTHERN ALPS

The Tasman Glacier ski-field is not, as one might think, a fast, downhill run, but rather something of a ski journey over slopes of varying steepness, traversing flats and mounds, for a distance of about 8km (5 miles). It is principally a wonderful wander amongst magnificent alpine scenery – but the guides recommend it only for experienced skiers.

RIGHT: HOOKER GLACIER, SOUTHERN ALPS

The Empress, Noeline and Mona Glaciers, pushing down from Endeavour Col on the Mt Cook Range, are brought up short by the high wall of rock where the Baker Saddle climbs between La Perouse and the lesser Dilemma Peak. Not to be denied, they swing southward, combining into one great ice-fall, the Hooker Glacier, comparatively short, steep and spectacular.

LEFT: TUI TARN, CASS RIVER, MACKENZIE COUNTRY

There are two Cass Rivers in Canterbury – but to trampers of the bare, almost sub-antarctic upland of the Mackenzie, the better-known Cass River is the one which runs down from a high valley between the Liebig and Hall Ranges to Lake Tekapo. Though its domain is bare and windswept, it possesses the lonely, wild glory reflected in the still, cold waters of Tui Tarn.

RIGHT: LINDIS PASS HILLS

The Lindis Pass, where a narrow, dusty road slips through from the Mackenzie Basin to Central Otago, is a place of snow and floods in winter, and of oven-like heat in summer, when the hills are baked brown and resemble the folds of a carelessly dropped blanket. The Lindis Pass was known to the pre-European Maori, who wandered frequently over its 1006m (3300ft) altitude.

BELOW RIGHT: LAKE OHAU, MACKENZIE COUNTRY

Like other lakes of glacial origin, Ohau is surrounded by superb mountain scenery, the high, snow-covered ranges rising from the water's edge; and close to the tourist lodge, which sits on this broad shelf overlooking the lake, is a fine ski-field. Ohau is the southernmost of the Mackenzie Country lakes, and perhaps the most spectacular, being more like the alpine lakes of Central Otago than are Tekapo, Pukaki or Alexandrina. At an altitude of 524m (1720ft), Ohau spreads over 60 square km (23 square miles).

OVER PAGE: PURAKAUNUI FALLS, SOUTH OTAGO

Purakaunui Falls, in the Catlins District of South Otago, is an exquisite cascade set in a tract of native forest, on steeply falling land near the coast. Easily reached by a walkway from the road, the falls are rapidly becoming a premier tourist attraction. (Though the setting is beautiful, the name has unpleasant associations. It means 'big stack of firewood', and is a contemptuous reference to the bodies of Maori warriors slain in an ancient tribal battle, and stacked ready for cooking and eating.)

ABOVE: TREE FERN FRONDS

In the Westland rain forests, at the feet of the high Alps, on that narrow shelf between the mountains and the sea, the tree ferns grow to prodigious size, their budding, violin-neck fronds opening out, palm-tree-like, to sway and wave along the roadsides at the edge of the dark bush. Such fronds are a frequent element in the art of the Maori carver.

RIGHT: LAKE HAWEA, OTAGO

Lake Hawea, lying in the bed of a prehistoric glacier, is some 124 square km (48 square miles) in area – 35km (22 miles) long and up to 8km (5 miles) wide. Magnificently overlooked by the range which runs between Mt Grandview and Dingle Peak, the lake has that frequently found quality of mirror stillness which seems to be characteristic of lakes of glacial origin; and when the dusk gathers early, as it does in such deep mountain valleys, the high, still-daylit clouds are reflected perfectly in the glassy water, giving back a second-hand light which holds back the darkness on the valley floor for a little while longer.

TOP LEFT: BULLER RIVER AT LAKE ROTOROA, NELSON LAKES DISTRICT

Where the main alpine chain spreads out at its northern end into a fantastic tangle of complicated ranges, in a region criss-crossed with deep rift valleys, lie Lakes Rotoiti and Rotoroa, set like jewels in the forested mountains. From Lake Rotoroa, the larger of the two, issues the Buller River, lusty and powerful and deep right from its source and all the way down to the Tasman Sea.

BELOW LEFT: UPPER WAIRAU RIVER, MARLBOROUGH

The Wairau River begins in a long fold in the crumpled country east of the Spenser Mountains. It tumbles down through high-altitude beech forests into a fern and tussock basin beneath Mt Alma, and swings sharply northward, to brawl and foam beneath the eastern faces of the St Arnaud Range, before flowing on its way to the Pacific Ocean.

ABOVE: UPPER WAIMAKARIRI, CANTERBURY

The upper reaches of the Waimakariri (Cold Waters) River, where it wanders out from the high alps, are a tangled skein of gravel-choked waterways, subject to sudden floods when the snows melt or there are heavy rains in the mountain valleys. The Waimakariri, like the Rangitata and the Rakaia, waters the broad Canterbury Plain, which, indeed, these mountain-bred rivers helped to form, by bringing gravels down from the mountainsides and depositing them in the shallow sea which once washed the skirts of the foothills.

LEFT: LAKE MARIAN AND MT CROSSCUT

Tucked into the folds of the mountains at the head of the Maria Valley in the Hollyford region of Fiordland, Lake Marian lies below the Lyttle Falls, which leap down from a hanging valley holding two more small lakes. The valley runs east-west between the precipitous and imposing faces of Mt Christine and Mt Crosscut. A Surveyor-General, E.H. Wilmot, chose to bestow the name of a young cousin on this almost overpowering area. Not only did he name the valley after her, but also the sublime little lake, plus two lakes near the head of the falls, which he named Mariana and Marianette, a dainty nomenclature for such a powerful landscape.

ABOVE: CRAIGIEBURN SKI-FIELD

On the road that leads from Christchurch to Arthur's Pass, there are some fine ski-fields, mostly operated by ski clubs – family fields, a mere hour and a half by car from Christchurch. The Craigieburn field has a rope tow and other essential facilities; nothing large or opulent, but enough to ensure skiers of all levels of skills – competitive skiers, fun skiers and complete novices – a good day's fun for a good price. Pines have been planted on the slopes in this area, to hold together slopes which, when not under snow, erode massively.

Order Amongst Natural Beauty

EVEN surrounded by a superabundance of natural beauty, people still have other needs. Man might not live by bread alone, but bread he must have to live at all. So the landscape is drilled and marshalled until it functions like machinery, to feed and clothe and house humankind. Also, though there are a few exceptional people for whom the untamed wilderness is all they need, there are many more for whom wild beauty is better taken in small sips. Most people, though they enjoy the grandeur of mountains and the riotous growth of the bush, have a need for ordered paths, tidy lawns and disciplined, flowery gardens.

In addition, those brave souls who first abandoned their familiar scenery to settle in a new and alien land experienced a crushing homesickness. To alleviate its very real pain, they hastened to establish in their new situation the style of buildings, the trees, flowers, animals and birds they had known and loved in the Old Country.

Yet it could never be a real duplication. For one thing, there was so much more land to spare. Farms were measured in thousands of acres, sheep runs in hundreds of square miles, rather than the neat, small, intensely cultivated holdings of rural England, measured in fifties or hundreds of acres. Every householder was encouraged to build his home on a half-acre or quarter-acre section, with the result that populations which would have fitted easily into a small cluster of semi-detached cottages bordering a quarter of a mile of English road, here sprawled over a square mile of perfectly farmable landscape; and the larger centres sprawled outward over areas that would have contained an English city.

Even architecture could not entirely reproduce the familiar English scene. The traditional methods of building were not entirely suitable. Nogging, for example, that style of building which is usually labelled 'Tudor', though it is much older than that, consisting of an exposed framing with the bricks laid in between the frame members, proved unsatisfactory in New Zealand because of the ferocious shrinkage of New Zealand timbers. The stone houses and ecclesiastical buildings which, in England, stood for centuries, could not cope with the earthquakes of this geologically younger land. So architecture and building practices became a sort of compromise, out of which grew some original and striking innovations.

LILY GIGANTUM, MT PEEL HOMESTEAD GROUNDS, CANTERBURY
Old World trees and Old World wildflowers create an English woodland in country which must have seemed, to the first Mt Peel settlers, to be a dreary, alien, tussock-covered wilderness at the feet of the overbearing mountains.

ABOVE: THE CHRISTCHURCH TOWN HALL AND FERRIER FOUNTAIN

On the banks of the principal stream, the settlers' descendants built their Town Hall complex, purely New Zealand in its architecture, yet somehow as English as a medieval castle. And in its courtyard, to offset its severity, they set fountains like giant thistledown.

RIGHT: DAFFODILS, BOTANICAL GARDENS, CHRISTCHURCH

On a swampy site, in heavy soil laced with a network of peaty streams, the Canterbury pioneers built a city. In its midst, they reserved 200 hectares (497 acres) of hard-won ground, to serve as a park and a garden, so that city dwellers would never lack for outdoor spaces; and in the middle of the park, they planted a garden of English trees, and patched the greensward with beds of daffodils so that spring in the heart of Christchurch would always remind them of April in England ...

ABOVE: CHRISTCHURCH CATHEDRAL AND CATHEDRAL SQUARE

At the city's heart, they raised a Gothic cathedral, to denote the nature of their settlement and the direction of their own ideals. For the Canterbury pioneers were principally a Church of England band, and the Church originally undertook their pastoral and educational care. It was planned from the first that Christchurch should have a public school (English style) and a university; and the university chapel was to double as a cathedral. Circumstances changed these schemes somewhat, but the Christchurch Cathedral was built where the school and university were to have stood – in the centre of the city.

Some native trees did provide exceptionally fine building timbers; but the best of such timbers were slow-growing; and, moreover, early exploitation brought at least one species to the verge of extinction. Certain exotic trees, notably the radiata pine, were found to grow rapidly and well – so now vast areas have been planted in geometrically rectangular stands, tidily separated into dark green regiments by access roads and fire-breaks.

The rivers which flow mightily down to the ocean from upland lake and permanent snowfield have proved to be eminently harnessable for the production of electric power, or the irrigation of otherwise waste areas, or both. This has resulted in the creation of vast lakes, with resultant changes in weather patterns over certain areas.

LEFT: THE CANTERBURY PLAINS

The patchwork that is the Canterbury Plains has been created by heroic amounts of sheer hard work – meticulously straight fencelines, the careful rotating of crop and pasture, and the dark lines of pine and macrocarpa windbreaks, planted to protect the light, silty topsoil from the boisterous nor'west winds.

ABOVE: TIMARU HARBOUR AND WHARVES

To create a port out of a shallow indentation in Canterbury's Pacific coast took prodigious nineteenth-century engineering, with horse and dray, wheelbarrow, pick and shovel, steam-winches and primitive explosives. This port now provides an outlet point for the abundant produce of richly alluvial plains and the fertile, rolling hills of hinterland. Lyttelton, on Banks Peninsula, was always the principal Canterbury port, but in the days before the treacherous Rakaia and Rangitata Rivers were adequately bridged, another means of exporting seasonal produce had to be found. Timaru therefore became established as a port, and prospered.

OVER PAGE: OTAGO PENINSULA

There is an echo of old Scotland in the dry-stone fences, the sheltering clumps of wind-sculpted trees, the occasional blaze of gorse and the tidy houses and barns of the Otago Peninsula. It lies alongside a harbour which is like a long and narrow loch. A mere stone's throw from the city of Dunedin, the peninsula is considered to be in it, but is not really of it, being a different world entirely from the busy city across the harbour.

ABOVE: MARLBOROUGH VINEYARD

Rows of vines march steadily towards the Inland Kaikoura Ranges seen here in the background. Marlborough is one of the sunniest regions in the country and all this sunshine – along with the variety of soil types, long autumns and crisp, cool winters – has made it the country's largest wine-growing region. Although the Marlborough wine-making industry has only been going since the 1970s, it has developed at an extraordinary rate. Its reputation for producing excellent wines, sauvignon blanc in particular, is now internationally acknowledged.

ABOVE RIGHT: NELSON, FROM QUEBEC ROAD

Nelson nestles about the curve of its bay, with hills rising steeply at its back – a thriving centre for the richly fertile valleys in the folds of the northern ranges. Once – and perhaps still – a favourite retirement spot because of its gently warm climate, it is today a thriving and busy city, surrounded by an intriguing mix of modern industrial complexes and cottage industries.

BELOW RIGHT: PINE FOREST, WHANGAMOA, NELSON

Vast acreages of pine, regimentally aligned, clothe the slopes of the high hills of Nelson Province, providing timber and, incidentally, holding firmly together slopes which would otherwise erode massively. Pine chips from the region have become a significant export, contributing handsomely to the whole country's economy.

PREVIOUS PAGE, LEFT: ALPINE NIGHT, QUEENSTOWN AND LAKE WAKATIPU

There are lights that twinkle across the Frankton Arm of Lake Wakatipu when the daylight fails and the frost chills the evening air in Queenstown. In Queenstown itself, for most of the year, the languages and accents of almost every country in the world can be heard, as tourists flock here in summer and autumn for the sightseeing, and in winter and early spring for the magnificent skiing.

PREVIOUS PAGE, BELOW: ARROWTOWN

When autumn colours the avenue in Arrowtown, the cosy cottages built by the nineteenth-century goldminers come into their own, being small, for easy heating, and touchingly home-like. The town was built during the goldrush of the 1860s and the town centre has altered little since then. The first-comers won more than 200lb (100kg) of gold in the first few weeks in this area.

PREVIOUS PAGE ABOVE: OLD COACHING INN, SKIPPERS ROAD, QUEENSTOWN

The old inn remembers the days when the modern 20-minute drive over good roads between Queenstown and Arrowtown was an arduous, punishing day's travel by pack-train or, later, two or three hours' journey by coach.

ABOVE LEFT: QUEENSTOWN,
LAKE WAKATIPU AND WALTER PEAK

Lovely Queenstown is a garden built and flourishing upon what was once a tumble of rock, the terminal moraine of a glacier. A colourful town with a colourful past, the centre is still clustered around its little, square bay and its miniature wharves as though, like its former inhabitants used to do, it is still welcoming boatloads of gold prospectors arriving from Kingston, at the lake's southern end.

ABOVE: ARROW BASIN, NEAR
QUEENSTOWN

Even the killing frosts of winter and the broiling suns of summer have not prevented farmers from planting and cultivating the hard Arrow Basin country. As the gold-seekers crowded into these wild mountain valleys, farmers also came – not to gamble on finding fortunes in gold, but settling for the certainty that the miners would need food, and that farmers and farms would still be needed when all the gold had gone.

LEFT: OTAGO PENINSULA RURAL SCENE

The afternoon sun that touches the old volcanic rim of Otago Peninsula lights a scene of pastoral peace, where sheep graze about the ancient, towering lava plugs; for, like Lyttelton to the north, Otago Harbour is a drowned volcanic crater, and ancient lava spillings form reefs along its eastern shore. The peninsula is almost parallel to the mainland shore, forming the eastern wall of a long, narrow harbour with one winding, dredged, deep-water channel which was contrived to bring ships to the commercial heart of Dunedin.

BELOW: DUNEDIN

Dunedin, often called 'the Edinburgh of the South', is home to many fine examples of Victorian architecture such as the Law Courts seen here.

LEFT: HEREFORD CATTLE, LAKE HAWEA, OTAGO

Along the western shore of Lake Hawea, beneath the frowning peaks, a broad shelf of land is a sheltered Shangri-La, where fine Hereford cattle graze and grow fat. On these 'flats', in days gone by, cereal crops were grown, of such fine quality that buyers were attracted from all over the country.

ABOVE LEFT: ACHERON ACCOMMODATION HOUSE, MARLBOROUGH

The early settlers found the tussock-covered hills of Marlborough's high country ideal for sheep. But for sheep there had to be shepherds and drovers, and for them there had to be shelter against the potentially lethal high-country weather.

Accommodation houses were built, such as this one at Acheron, near the head of the Clarence River. In this virtually treeless region, the house had to be built of the very ground on which it stands, of cob, which is a puddled mixture of clay, chopped tussock and chaff.

ABOVE: SHEEP, LAKE JOHNSON, OTAGO

Near Lake Johnson, sheep thrive in a similar green and unexpected oasis. Lake Johnson is a small lake near Lake Hayes, in the Wakatipu region. Its principal claim to fame is the fine trout fishing it affords, both brown and rainbow trout being caught in its still and sheltered waters. The lake's surroundings are not in the least typical of the rugged Central Otago landscape, being rolling green downs, more typical of South Canterbury or coastal Otago.

ABOVE: BENMORE HYDRO DAM AND LAKE

Forty years after Lake Mahinerangi was formed, in an immensely larger undertaking, engineers raised an earth dam between two hills near Otematata, behind which the Waitaki River backs up to fill the twisting, deep valleys. Benmore is one of the largest earth dams in the world. It stands 110m (360ft) high, 1219m (4000ft) long. Its lake covers 83 square km (32 square miles) with 160km (100 miles) of shoreline and 17 islands.

RIGHT: EVENING LIGHT, LAKE MAHINERANGI, OTAGO

Where once a simple hill-country stream wriggled down through Waipori Gorge, near Dunedin, engineers in the early years of the twentieth century built a dam, forming an artificial lake to store water for the Waipori Electric Power Stations. It was named Mahinerangi, not after some legendary Maori princess, but after the daughter of Dunedin's (1911) Mayor.

ABOVE: MOLESWORTH CATTLE DRIVE, MARLBOROUGH

The largest farm in New Zealand is the Molesworth Station, in the Marlborough highlands. During the summer cattle muster over the station's 180 000 hectares (445 000 acres) the cattle are driven along steep ridges, over wild river flats and down through the high passes to Culverden sales yards, where the mob is held, to be shipped by truck to Christchurch. This land was once divided into three vast sheep stations, but the land was eaten out and burnt over too hard, too frequently. It became infested with rabbits, its hillsides eroded and the whole area was seemingly ruined for livestock production. The Government took it over and it was gradually restored and stocked with cattle. Today it serves as a research station for high-country farming and tour operators take groups there for a taste of station life.

RIGHT: LAKE TEKAPO LANDSCAPE, MACKENZIE COUNTRY

The same fierce heat that scorches the Canterbury Plains is unrelieved over much of the Mackenzie Basin because of the sparsity of shade trees. But it ripens vast acreages of hay, to be mown and stored in huge, round bales, against the hungry winter. For, at an altitude of over 700m (2300ft), Lake Tekapo's climatic severity poses special problems in the maintenance of livestock in the cold months.

Many Canterbury runs were taken up by Australian graziers, who brought with them a better knowledge of farming in a dry, drought-prone country than the English farmers possessed. But it was the English who contrived to irrigate around 1 million hectares ($2^1/_2$ million acres) with water-race systems run from Canterbury's biggest rivers, and increased the land's sheep-carrying capacity dramatically. Today, a significant part of New Zealand's overall earnings comes from the export of wool and prime lamb carcasses from this area.

165

LEFT: SOUTH CANTERBURY RURAL SCENE

Around the edges of the Canterbury Plains, where the hills begin to rise towards the mountains, pleasant rural dales, hedged and green and shaded with trees, contrast with the wilder hills beyond. There tends to be a fairly sharp demarcation between the rolling pastures of the lower foothills and the sudden heights and bush-clad steeps of the sub-alpine ranges. It is a contrast which dramatically accentuates the ordered neatness of those hills which have been brought under cultivation.

ABOVE LEFT: HARVESTING, CANTERBURY PLAINS

The patchwork of the Canterbury Plains is composed of alternating fields of pasture, fodder crops and cereal crops, including barley, oats and wheat, with sowings of winter feed for sheep, all separated by fences. Originally (in that treeless expanse), walls of sods were raised as fences, and were planted on top with gorse hedges, stockproof and dense enough to give growing crops some measure of shelter.

ABOVE: PASTORAL SCENE NEAR WAIKARI, NORTH CANTERBURY

Waikari, Hawarden and Culverden are three small communities set in a rolling upland basin walled about with high ranges. Green and fertile, based on great reefs of limestone, the countryside is ideal for sheep. The little townships bask in the sunshine of long summers, and are snugly sited and hospitable when the high-altitude winters bring snow and crackling frosts.

Victory of the Sea

THERE is no particular or mystical quality about the Tasman Sea or the Pacific Ocean that would give a unique character to either of the coasts they have shaped along the flanks of the South Island. Both seas attack the shore with equal ferocity, or roll up to it in precisely the same kind of long swell, with a mighty surf where the continental shelf resists the in-rushing water, or with a long, swift tidal rip where an offshore current races around the turn of a headland and gouges an adjacent sweep of shore.

True, the Pacific coast has miles-long stretches of fine, sandy beach – but the Tasman coast has its Punakaiki, almost tropical under the caress of a warm current, with tall and graceful nikau palms, and the jungle-like bush coming down to the shore. True, the Tasman coast has its wild and rocky headlands – but the Pacific coast has the Kaikoura coast, with reef-guarded coves, romantically rock-bound capes and stern peninsulas at whose feet the bull kelp swirls and the incoming tides crash against granite cliffs.

It is the land, the magnificent, overpowering, high-reaching land that seems to marshal the sea and command its currents, deciding the shape of its own shores.

It's an ancient warfare, this battle between ocean and island. Here and there are traces of the sea's victory, as at the northern end of the island, where a gigantic subsidence between Marlborough's seaward ranges and the distant coast of the South Taranaki Bight has left a network of drowned valleys forming the Marlborough Sounds; or where the ocean has breached the walls of volcanic craters to form the harbours of Lyttelton, Akaroa and Dunedin. Here and there the land has been victorious, as where its rivers, bringing down gravel from the mountains, built up the Canterbury Plain until it reached out and snared the island which became Banks Peninsula.

In places, the coastline runs across the end of the mountain ranges, to form a rugged shore deeply indented with bays and coves and land-locked havens, or deeply gashed with fiords. Elsewhere, the plains and coastward hills terminate abruptly in high cliffs, at whose bases narrow shingle beaches are pounded by ocean rollers along steeply shelving shores. And where rivers run out between sheltering headlands, beaches have built up – handsome sweeps of sand, backed sometimes by bush and sometimes by dunes, pale blue-green with marram grass and lupins.

LEFT: SUNRISE, LYTTELTON HARBOUR

The early sun, peeping over the rim of the drowned volcanic crater which forms Lyttelton Harbour, wakens the small, pleasant, tree-shaded harbourside settlements. Lyttelton Harbour was to have been the site of Canterbury's principal city, and was named in honour of Lord Lyttelton, the Chairman of the Canterbury Association. But the site proved to be too cramped and too short of fresh water, beneath those basalt walls.

PREVIOUS PAGE: MITRE PEAK, MILFORD SOUND

The massive peaks which tower over Milford Sound rise sheer from the cold, clear water to heights of over 1500m (5000ft), and it is their prodigious height which makes the Sound seem narrow, though it is actually up to 5km (3 miles) wide.

RIGHT: THE OTAGO COAST NORTH OF TAIERI MOUTH, OTAGO

The South Otago coast, north of Taieri Mouth, runs in successive crescents of sandy beach, swept clean by the sea currents.

ABOVE: STEWART ISLAND/RAKIURA, VIEWED FROM COSY NOOK, SOUTHLAND

Cosy Nook, on the southern coast of the South Island, is somewhat protected by its guardian rocks and reefs from the boisterous Foveaux Strait. Across the strait there is a distant view of Stewart Island/Rakiura, with its darkly forested ranges and sharply conical Mt Anglem.

ABOVE: ERNEST ISLAND, STEWART ISLAND/
RAKIURA

The magnificent Port Pegasus harbour is on
the southern side of Stewart Island/Rakiura.
Its South Arm is guarded from the ocean
swell by a great hump of land indented
with coves. Even on the lee side of this
hump, anchorages have names like
Disappointment Cove and Fright Cove,
which may give some idea of the sudden
violence of the seas in these parts. On the
windward side, it is hardly surprising to find
tiny Ernest Island, standing in the mouth of
a long, deep inlet, marked on the charts as
a 'small craft retreat'. But Ernest Island itself
is a peacefully idyllic knob of land, with
bird-loud bush, and a tree-fringed, curving
bay on its own leeside.

There are beaches that stand behind rocky reefs and gaze out across cold,
southern waters towards the far, ice-bound seas of Antarctica, far beyond the rim
of the horizon. There are beaches that are windswept and wild and strewn with
driftwood. There are even beaches that are a rock-hound's delight, strewn with
gemstones deposited by currents which tore them from volcanic cliffs. There are
beaches which sit at a city's feet, with neat lawns behind them and a safe, sandy-
bottomed bay lapping at them with gentle tides.

The character of the South Island's coastline is infinitely varied, abounding in
inlets and indentations that make it a small-boat navigator's paradise. Rich in
scenic variety, and dotted with natural wonders such as odd rock formations,
blowholes, caves, cruel reefs and the white smile of long curves of surf, it is never
far from any New Zealander's door – and it is by no means the least of the South
Island's magnificent scenic attractions.

BELOW: TOKO MOUTH, SOUTH OTAGO

The Toko Stream meanders down to a sandy coast through a reedy, scrub-patched fen, to spill into a bay of calm beauty, gently shelving and safe, where South Otago people have built the holiday homes to which they bring their children for the long summer holidays. An ocean current which seeps along this coast maintains a water temperature of around 15.6°C (60°F) all year round.

RIGHT: COASTAL CLIFFS NEAR KAITANGATA, SOUTH OTAGO

South of Toko Mouth, the uprising land stands above the Pacific Ocean atop tall cliffs of crumbly-looking conglomerate which, nevertheless, is as hard as concrete and is seamed, in the vicinity of Kaitangata, with coal. The coast abounds in fish, and several fleets of small fishing boats operate just offshore, and have their anchorages in river mouths and headland-protected bays.

PREVIOUS PAGE: SOUTHLAND DAWN,
RIVERTON

At the western extremity of the sandy curve
of bay between Invercargill's Oreti Beach
and the township of Riverton, Howells Point
thrusts eastward, a sheltering spearpoint of
a headland, making the estuary of the
Aparima and Pourakino Rivers a secure
anchorage for fishing boats which operate
in the stormy waters of Foveaux Strait.

LEFT: OAMARU HARBOUR AND
CAPE WANBROW

Oamaru Harbour, sheltered from the
southerly winds by Cape Wanbrow, was
once a busy coastal port. With the decline
of coastal shipping, it has become a haven
for a fishing fleet. The harbour – and the
town – occupy yet another ancient volcanic
crater.

RIGHT: KARITANE COAST, OTAGO

The Karitane Coast must be one of the most
idyllic spots in New Zealand, with its
curving, sandy, gently shelving beaches and
its romantic peninsula, all backed by a
story-book countryside of tidy, green farms.
Here, too, small boats form an offshore
fishing fleet, anchoring in the shelter of the
peninsula between fishing sweeps.

LEFT: THE MOERAKI BOULDERS,
NORTH OTAGO

Moeraki Beach, on North Otago's coast, is
strewn with these round stones, which
seem to have formed around a crystalline
centre over aeons of time, much as a pearl
forms around a piece of grit in an oyster
shell. In Maori lore, the stones are sweet
potatoes and gourds, the cargo of a
wrecked ancestral canoe.

ABOVE: PUNAKAIKI SEASCAPE

The Tasman Sea coast can be wild, lonely
and magnificently moody. The beach south
of Punakaiki and north of Greymouth, with
its foaming breakers and its salt-laden haze,
is typical of much of the South Island's
west-coast scenery. A warm current just
offshore transforms the coastal hills in this
area into a tropical jungle, even to the
fringe of nikau palms that nod and sway
above the beaches.

**RIGHT: EARLY MORNING SCENE, EAST
COAST OF STEWART ISLAND/RAKIURA**

Though Stewart Island/Rakiura possesses
luxuriant forests, and the coves and sandy
beaches seem to belong to a tropical isle, it
still manages, at certain times and in certain
lights, to convey a reminder that it is, after
all, the last outpost, the final dot of
habitable land, between the main islands
and the Antarctic.

LEFT: THE PANCAKE ROCKS, PUNAKAIKI

Close to the mouth of the Porari River, the turbulent sea has pounded and gouged and carved a headland into a fantastic semblance of piles of great, grey pancakes. It is awe-inspiring to stand on the ground in this area and feel it tremble to the surge and suck of the sea in long caverns beneath your feet. Here and there, pockets of air compressed at the end of such caverns by the in-rushing water have burst through the cavern roofs, forming blowholes through which great geysers of seawater jet high into the air.

ABOVE RIGHT: JACKSON BAY, SOUTH WESTLAND

Farther south, where the sea reaches almost to the feet of the Alps, its waters seem subdued, lapping gently at the narrow beaches. But even here storms can send the sea crashing right to the foot of the Jackson Bay cliffs. There is a wharfage for coastal vessels here, and the bay has long been a minor port, though of much diminished importance now that roads from the north and the east reach Haast and the cattle runs in this 'frontier' area.

BELOW RIGHT: PORARI RIVERMOUTH, PUNAKAIKI COAST

Where the Porari River rumbles down from the hills to the Punakaiki coast, and sweeps out across the sand through a gap in the rugged cliffs, a fine, sandy beach has established itself. This part of the west coast is a favourite holiday spot, beautiful, and sheltered by high spurs. Its beaches are gently shelving and safe.

LEFT: TAHUNANUI BEACH, NELSON

Throughout Nelson's long, hot summers, Tahunanui Beach on the shores of Tasman Bay is crowded with sunloving humanity; but as evening closes in, the oyster catchers and stilts and gulls reassert their ancient ownership as they feed in the wake of a receding tide.

ABOVE: TARAKOHE COAST, GOLDEN BAY, NELSON

The marble hills of Takaka slope down to the Tarakohe coast on the eastern shores of Golden Bay, that rocky and often spectacular seaboard. In 1642, Abel Tasman called it 'Murderers' Bay', because Maori warriors attacked one of his small boats and killed four of his crew. Today it is known as Golden Bay, and its climate and deeply indented, attractive coast are well described by such a warm and pleasant title.

ABOVE: PICTON, MARLBOROUGH SOUNDS

It is difficult to realise that Picton, spilling down the slopes from the foot of the bush-clad ranges, is the South Island terminal of the ferry link between the two islands. Once Wellington's rival as proposed seat of Government, the little town at the head of Queen Charlotte Sound remains a tranquil holiday resort, linked to the workaday south by thin ribbons of road and rail through the protecting hills.

RIGHT: MAORI LEAP CAVES, KAIKOURA

The Maori Leap Caves, near Kaikoura, in limestone cliffs once hammered by the sea, now stand well back from the shore, eerie caverns hung with stalactites dripping like spilled toffee. In their dark corners the ancient bones of seal and penguin are hidden among the forgotten ocean flotsam of lime-encrusted driftwood and empty shells.

ABOVE: KAIKOURA

The little town of Kaikoura, on the east coast, is spread out above a steeply shelving, shingly beach. The pleasant bay is protected by arms of rocky reef and stubby peninsula. In the bay, seals fish alongside men in the long ocean swell; and over all leans the lofty Seaward Kaikoura Range. Here, within one small area, is a microcosmic view of the essential South Island – mountain, forest, farm and shore.

ABOVE: TENNYSON INLET, MARLBOROUGH SOUNDS

Tennyson Inlet, branching southward from the land-locked waterway known as Tawhitinui Reach, is typical of the Marlborough Sounds – deep, well sheltered and watched over by brown, forest-patched hills. A sizeable navy could anchor in this network of waterways, but most of the traffic upon these sheltered reaches consists of pleasure boats and the launches which serve otherwise isolated farms.

RIGHT: OKURI BAY AND D'URVILLE ISLAND, MARLBOROUGH SOUNDS

An ancient and cataclysmic subsidence once plunged a landscape of dovetailing spurs and high ridges deep beneath the waters of the South Taranaki Bight. The hills above Okuri Bay and the rugged spurs of D'Urville Island were once the peaks of continuous ranges, now drowned beneath the blue waters of French Pass.

LEFT: MT SHEWELL AND FITZROY BAY, MARLBOROUGH SOUNDS

Fitzroy Bay is a complex harbour with many coves and inlets. A long spur from Mt Shewell, 775m (2542ft), runs down to Sheep Point, northern head of the almost land-locked bay. The hills, and the mountain itself, like most Marlborough Sounds countryside, are sun-browned pastures grazed by sheep, and patched with exotic and native forest.

ABOVE: WHARAIKI BEACH, CAPE FAREWELL

Wharaiki Beach, on the western side of Cape Farewell, looks out, past the offshore rocks, across the stormy Tasman Sea. The region is known for its beautiful sunsets. Cape Farewell was the last land sighted by Captain James Cook as he departed from New Zealand after his first exploratory voyage around the coast, and set sail for Australia.

ABOVE: KAIKOURA COAST

The Inland and the Seaward Kaikoura
Ranges run straight, parallel courses then
drop down abruptly to the sea, south of
where the Clarence River pours out from its
high valleys. The coast here is a rugged
rock-bound shore of jagged reefs and
swirling kelp. Like England's Cornish coast,
or the stormy coast of Maine, it is a place of
deep little inlets where the crayfish, from
which it gets its name (Kaikoura means
'feast of crayfish'), are still abundant.

This edition published in 1999 by New Holland Kowhai
an imprint of New Holland Publishers (NZ) Ltd
Auckland • Sydney • London • Cape Town

218 Lake Road, Northcote, Auckland, New Zealand
14 Aquatic Drive, Frenchs Forest, NSW 2086, Australia
86–88 Edgware Road, London W2 2EA, United Kingdom
80 McKenzie Street, Cape Town 8001, South Africa

Copyright © 1999 New Holland Publishers (NZ) Ltd
Copyright © in photographs: Warren Jacobs and Robin Smith, with
  the exception of p 50: Gareth Eyres; pp 51, 64, 147, 159: David Wall
Copyright © 1999 in maps: New Holland Publishers (NZ) Ltd
Copyright © 1999 in Mountain High Maps™ 1993 Digital Wisdom Inc

First published in 1988 by Kowhai Publishing Ltd

ISBN 1 877246 12 3

Cover design: Errol McLeary
Design: Barbara Nielsen

Printed in China through Colorcraft Ltd., Hong Kong

10 9 8 7 6 5